WHEN THE PIECES DON'T FIT

WHEN THE PIECES DON'T FIT

Making Sense of the Puzzles of Faith

Karen Mason

Discovery House Publishers

Books, music, and videos that feed the soul with the Word of God

Box 3566 Grand Rapids, MI 49501

Discovery House Publishers is affiliated with RBC Ministries,
Grand Rapids, Michigan.

Discovery House books are distributed to the trade exclusively by
Barbour Publishing, Inc., Uhrichsville, Ohio.

Requests for permission to quote from this book should be directed to:
Permissions Department, Discovery House Publishers, P.O. Box 3566,
Grand Rapids, MI 49501.

Scripture quotations are from the *Holy Bible, New International
Version®*. *NIV®*. Copyright © 1973, 1978, 1984 by International Bible
Society. Used by permission of Zondervan. All rights reserved.

Interior design by Julie Ackerman Link

Library of Congress Cataloging-in-Publication Data
Available on request

Printed in the United States of America

08 09 10 11 12 13 14 15 / DKN / 10 9 8 7 6 5 4 3 2 1

CONTENTS

INTRODUCTION

MY FIANCÉ FELT PUZZLED. THE TWO OF US HAD AGREED that we wanted to live a simple lifestyle, but after we were engaged I told him that I wanted a full set of china. My two statements were confusing to him, but they made sense to me. I remembered all the entertaining my parents had done with their china, and I wanted to be able to continue that kind of hospitality.

Sometimes we can feel the same kind of confusion in our relationship with God. We think we know Him, but then we find out that He isn't who we thought He was.

When I flunked calculus in college, I felt this way. I believed that good people obtain favor from the LORD (Proverbs 12:2) and that "no harm befalls the righteous" (Proverbs 12:21). I considered myself a righteous, good person, so I assumed that God would bring me success in college. I didn't know there was more to God than that simple thing. I didn't know that God also creates each of us specially and gives us opportunities to discover our uniqueness. As the psalmist David wrote,

> My frame was not hidden from you when I was made in the secret place. When I was woven together in the depths of the earth, your eyes saw my unformed body. All the days ordained for me were written in your book before one of them came to be. (Psalm 139:15–16)

Flunking calculus taught me something about myself: God created me with a brain that has limited ability to understand that subject. But I also learned that I didn't know God as well as I thought I did. I was confused about what He was doing.

When cell phones first came out, my friend's mom thought they could be used only in the car. So she would make calls from her car in the garage. She believed something, but that didn't make it true. I made the same mistake about God. I thought that believing something about God made it true.

EVERYONE HAS A THEOLOGY

Each of us has a set of beliefs about God that we think are true. These beliefs lead to certain expectations, and these beliefs and expectations become our "theology." Just as different people can have different experiences with the same person, so we all have different experiences with God. We develop theologies that fit our experiences.

When I was growing up, I said a prayer before eating: "God is good, God is great, thank you for this food. Amen." I had a vague notion that being good and great meant giving me open-faced peanut butter sandwiches with my name written in honey. I held onto this theology of God as being "really nice" until I found out that God didn't always come through according to my expectations in life's more challenging situations. When I flunked calculus, I had to start rethinking my theology. I had to match my experience of God with who He really was.

When a drunk driver killed my brother, I didn't understand why God didn't protect him. When a church I was attending struggled through leadership issues and the elders voted before hearing both sides, my faith in God's justice was shattered. When I began to encounter life's countless disappointments and difficulties, I knew I had to develop a new set of beliefs about God.

My rethinking began with reading the Bible for myself. In doing so, I kept bumping up against puzzling statements that seemed contradictory. In Jesus' first sermon, He said, "Blessed are the poor in spirit, for theirs is the kingdom of heaven" (Matthew 5:3).

How, I wondered, can a person be "poor in spirit" and be blessed, or "happy"? Later, Jesus said, "Be perfect, therefore, as your heavenly Father is perfect" (Matthew 5:48). But Paul seemed to contradict this when he wrote, "The only thing that counts is faith expressing itself through love" (Galatians 5:6).

God and the Bible were a big mystery to me. So I set out to learn more about God. Just as I had to learn more about the man who became my husband, I had to discover more about God in order to have an intimate relationship with Him. He calls us to love Him as He dearly loves us. To understand what this means, I had to make sense of what seemed contradictory.

This book is about our lifelong journey of understanding God, about getting to know Him better by understanding some of the puzzling contradictions we find in Scripture. Each chapter addresses a puzzle, a seeming contradiction, in the Bible.

- How can we have rights and also give them up?
- How can we be both sinful and wonderful?
- How can we be imperfect and yet strive for perfection?
- How can the world be evil when God is in control?
- How can we passively rely on God and actively make decisions?
- How can God use both our weaknesses and our strengths?
- How can we seek spiritual healing while also seeking physical healing?
- How can we have the power to serve others when we have no power?

Perhaps you are stuck in one of these puzzles of faith. Let's start looking at them and find out how the pieces fit together so we can complete the picture of our loving relationship with God.

LIFE'S CONFUSING PUZZLES

BLUE SKY

Opportunity seldom knocks twice.

Strike while the iron is hot.

He who hesitates is lost.

Do not answer a fool according to his folly, or you will be like him yourself. (Proverbs 26:4)

GREEN TREE

Look before you leap.

Fools rush in where angels fear to tread.

Better safe than sorry

Answer a fool according to his folly, or he will be wise in his own eyes. (Proverbs 26:5)

IMAGINE PUTTING TOGETHER A 500-PIECE PUZZLE of a cloudless blue sky reflected in a calm lake surrounded by green trees. You search and search for a blue piece for a section of the sky. Unable to find the piece that fits, you begin trying any piece on the table. To your surprise, the piece that fits is green. A tree branch was jutting into the sky right at that spot in the picture.

Sometimes life is like a confusing puzzle of blue sky and green tree pieces. God promises rest and yet sends trials. He promises that in losing our lives we'll gain them. He says the poor are rich. These pieces don't seem to fit. But is it possible that these concepts—like blue sky and green tree puzzle pieces—fit unexpectedly?

PROVERBS THAT DON'T SEEM TO FIT

Folk proverbs are like puzzle pieces that don't seem to fit. They capture truth, but usually only one side of it. For example, is it better to "look before you leap" or to "strike while the iron is hot"? It doesn't make sense that opposite ideas can both be true. Yet we know from experience that they are. Like blue sky and green tree pieces, they don't look as if they fit. But they do. If I'm at a garage sale and I find an antique plate that matches one I already have, I need to "strike while the iron is hot" because if I hesitate it will be lost. This opportunity won't knock twice. But if I'm looking for a house and I find one I like, I know it is prudent to have the home inspected for structural problems. I look before I leap. In fact, I'd be a fool to rush into that purchase. It's far better to be safe than sorry!

As the author of Ecclesiastes said, there is "a time to be silent and a time to speak, a time to love and a time to hate, a time for war and a time for peace" (3:7b–8). There is a time to "look before you leap" and a time to "strike while the iron is hot."

BIBLE PIECES THAT DON'T SEEM TO FIT

The Bible has many confusing concepts that are like blue sky and green tree puzzle pieces. In the book of Proverbs, we read, "Do not answer a fool according to his folly" (26:4). But the very next verse says, "Answer a fool according to his folly" (26:5). How can two statements that say opposite things fit together as part of one truth? Do we answer a fool according to his folly or not? The second part of verse 4 says, "or you will be like him yourself." The second part of verse 5 says, "or he will be wise in his own eyes." Verse 4 is telling us not to stoop to the level of a fool, whereas verse 5 is telling us that sometimes folly must be plainly exposed and denounced. Both proverbs are true, but neither is universal; they apply to different circumstances.

Jessica is a mean, middle-school girl who said to her classmate Sally, "We can't hang out with you. You stink!" If Sally answered by saying, "Well, you stink, too!" she would be answering folly with folly, and thus responding on Jessica's level. If Sally says nothing at all, Jessica will be wise in her own eyes. It would be better for Sally to answer Jessica according to her folly (that is, in a way Jessica can understand). Sally might say, "Now that I see how you act, I don't want to hang out with you."

The verses in Proverbs suggest that we should not answer

foolish people in the same way they talk to us, but in a way that points out their folly. The two pieces can be confusing until we realize that each captures one side of the same truth. Joined together, they solve an important life puzzle.

> The opposite of a correct statement is a false statement. But the opposite of a profound truth may well be another profound truth.
> (Niels Bohr, Danish physicist, 1885–1962)

COMMON PUZZLES

When the Bible or folk proverbs give conflicting advice, we have difficulty deciding which to follow. As a psychologist, I often work with people who get stuck between two pieces of a life puzzle.

"I'm so torn," said John. "My wife wants to move across town but my son doesn't want to leave our neighborhood and all his friends. If I make my wife happy, my son will be disappointed. I feel as if I have to choose between them, and I don't know what to do."

"I'm so depressed," said Steve. "I always wanted to be a coach, but my Dad had other ideas for me. He always wanted me to "make something" of myself, and coaching isn't what he had in mind. I'm miserable in my present job, but my Dad will be miserable if I quit my job and become a coach."

"I can't win," said Sara. "Either I take the promotion and make my friend jealous, or I keep the only good friend I have at work and make my boss mad—and maybe lose my job."

"My family is dysfunctional and my friends keep moving away," said Lisa. "I want friends, but if I get close to someone new, they'll just leave."

CHRISTIAN PUZZLES

In addition to life's common puzzles, the Bible introduces puzzles that can be even more troublesome. Jesus said, "If someone strikes you on the right cheek, turn to him the other also. . . . Give to the one who asks you, and do not turn away from the one who wants to borrow from you" (Matthew 5:39–42). Does this mean that when my neighbor borrows my new saw and doesn't return it, I can't ask for it back? Does Jesus mean that we give up all rights when we follow Him, or are there some rights that we retain? How do we solve this puzzle?

I have worked with many Christians who think that doing everything for everyone else is what Jesus always wants them to do. They think God requires them to love others and not themselves. They see their wants as being in conflict with God's, and they are certain that it is *either* their wants *or* God's. The very question "God *or* me?" assumes that Christians have to choose between two opposite thoughts.

EITHER–OR

I once saw a cartoon that showed a judge saying to jurors: "Your decision has to be either 'guilty' or 'not guilty.' I can't accept 'too close to call.'"

Like guilt and innocence, some things in life are "either-or." Either you're a male or you're a female. Either you're here or you're there. One is true and the other is false. The Old Testament story of two prostitutes (1 Kings 3:16–28) is an example of an "either-or" truth. Two women were claiming one son as their own. Solomon knew that only one of the women could be right, so he devised a clever test to determine the real mother.

There are many "either-or" truths for Christians. Either Jesus' sacrifice on the cross is enough for the forgiveness of our sins or it isn't. Either we serve God or we don't. Jesus said, "You cannot serve both God and Money" (Matthew 6:24). Either we live a life holy to God or we don't. Either we engage in the "acts of the sinful nature" or we live by "the fruit of the Spirit" (Galatians 5:19–23).

Many of us prefer either-or thinking. Like the judge, we want a clear verdict. Choosing one option is easier than balancing or blending two or more. We are more comfortable when we don't have to live in the tension of truths that seem contradictory. We prefer clear choices where one side is clearly true and the other side clearly is not.

Unfortunately, the Bible doesn't give clear "either-or" teaching in some areas. For example, we know that Jesus claimed to be God but He also was born human and He died human. Which is it? Is Jesus God or man? He is both. Jesus was one hundred percent God and one hundred percent man. But how can this be? These opposites don't seem to fit together.

What causes rain? Condensation or God? It's not either-or; it's both. God put the laws of nature in motion and keeps them going (Colossians 1:16–17). Both God and the laws of nature cause rain. Is a coin heads or tails? It's not one *or* the other; it's both. Heads *and* tails make up a single coin.

In his letter to believers in Rome, Paul wrote about Christians who disagreed as to what foods were acceptable to eat. Some refused to eat certain foods, and others maintained that "all food is clean" (Romans 14:20). Furthermore, some Christians considered certain days sacred whereas other Christians considered all days the same.

The important teaching in both regards is that we not judge others for their opinions and that we not cause immature believers to stumble in their Christian walk. Both teachings assume that it's okay to have different opinions and practices. Even though we prefer that only one side be true, some issues are not clear-cut. Some biblical teachings are like proverbs: they present opposing concepts and we're expected to resolve them. We're expected to figure out how blue sky and green tree pieces fit together.

> A man does not prove his greatness by standing at an extremity, but by touching both extremities at once and filling all that lies between them. (Blaise Pascal, *Pensées*)

BOTH–AND

Many puzzles are solved not by choosing one idea over another but by blending two ideas to form a third.[1]

Jesus often presented two sides of an issue without saying exactly how to harmonize them. For example, the Pharisees and the Herodians set up an "either-or" trap for Jesus when they asked Him if they should pay taxes to Caesar. The Pharisees were opposed to Roman rule and the Herodians supported Roman rule. They wanted to trap Jesus into betraying His allegiance either to Rome or to Israel so Jesus would get in trouble with at least one of their groups. Jesus solved their puzzle by saying: "Give to Caesar what is Caesar's, and to God what is God's" (Matthew 22:21). He did justice to both points of view by combining them in an unexpected way.

Another time Jesus said that "anyone who is angry with his brother will be subject to judgment" (Matthew 5:22). In a letter to believers in Ephesus, Paul laid out the other piece: "In your anger do not sin: Do not let the sun go down while you are still angry" (Ephesians 4:26). So is it okay to get angry? Do you have to choose either Jesus *or* Paul? Or can you solve the puzzle by agreeing that both statements are about resolving conflicts as soon as possible and not letting them grow into murderous thoughts and plans?

Jesus said, "Do not worry about your life, what you will eat or drink; or about your body, what you will wear" (Matthew 6:25). Christians in Thessalonica were living this out to the letter and not working or preparing for the future, so Paul said, "If a man will not work, he shall not eat" (2 Thessalonians 3:10). In other words, we shouldn't worry but we should work for what we eat and drink.

BOTH ARE TRUE AT DIFFERENT TIMES

The Platte River in Colorado has the reputation of being a mile wide and an inch deep. In summer, it's shallow. But in spring after a snowy winter, it flows deep. Depending on where you are and what time of year it is, the same river looks very different. The Platte River is both deep and shallow, depending on when and where you look at it.

This kind of both-and blend is found in the Bible too. Sex is both good and wrong; within marriage it is good; outside of marriage it is wrong (Exodus 20:14). Obedience to authorities is both good and wrong (Romans 13:1). Even non-Christian authorities are servants of God (v. 4) whom we are to obey. However, we do not have to obey if they tell us to stop preaching (Acts 5:29). And though Jesus did not defend himself to the authorities (Matthew 26:63), Paul did (Acts 24).

BOTH ARE TRUE AT THE SAME TIME

Seeming opposites can also be true at the same time. For example, rain comes from both condensation and from God. Health comes from medications and ultimately from God. We have been "predestined" to be adopted as God's sons (Ephesians 1:5), and God invites "whoever" to come to Him (John 3:16–18). We are saved by grace through faith, and "not by works" (Ephesians 2:8–9), and faith is dead unless accompanied by actions (James 2:17). We are free in Christ (Galatians 5:1), and "everything is permissible—but not everything is beneficial (1 Corinthians 10:23).

BLUE SKY	**GREEN TREE**
Condensation causes rain.	God causes rain.
Medicine cures disease.	God cures disease.
We are predestined to salvation.	God invites whomever to come to Him.
We are saved by faith alone.	Faith is dead without works.
We are free in Christ.	Not all things are beneficial.
Honor yourself.	Honor others.

NEITHER IS TRUE

When our family was climbing Mount Kilimanjaro in Africa, we overheard a Tanzanian guide discussing breakfast plans with some Italian climbers. The guide kept repeating, each time more loudly, "Do you want one hegg or two hegg?" One of the Italians kept repeating "No eggs please." Finally, the guide understood that neither of his two choices was acceptable to the climber.

I often work with clients who struggle to understand why God allowed something bad to happen to them. The either-or options they are working with go something like this. Either I can trust God because He shows His love in predictable ways. Or I can't trust God because He is unpredictable and sometimes seems to behave in unloving ways. These either-or opposites set up many Christians for losing their trust and faith in God when something bad happens to them. The reality is that neither of these opposites is true. The truth lies elsewhere—in God's incomprehensible love for us, which He may express in unexpected ways. Sometimes people need to look at the puzzle pieces differently. Sometimes their beliefs need to change.

BLENDING THE TRUTHS

A parable attributed to John Godfrey Saxe helps us understand the puzzle pieces of our lives. In Saxe's parable, one blind man touches the elephant's trunk and says the elephant is like a snake. Another blind man touches the elephant's knee and says the elephant is like a tree trunk. The third blind man touches the elephant's tail and says the elephant is like a rope. Each blind man was correct in describing one aspect of an elephant. But an elephant isn't only snake-like, trunk-like, or rope-like. An elephant is like all three. The seeming "opposites" have to be blended together to solve the puzzle.

Some issues in the Bible are similar. They seem to have two sides that are both true. These are most likely both-and puzzles. For example, the Bible is clear that Jesus is both human (Romans 5:17) and divine (Matthew 26:63–64; Philippians 2:6). These look like opposites but the Bible insists that both are true simultaneously. There are cults that do not blend the opposites and throw out one side or the other. For example, Mormonism teaches that Jesus was not God. Christians harmonize the seeming opposites: Jesus is both God and Man. It is the same with the Trinity. It is clear in the Bible that God is both One (Deuteronomy 6:4) and Three (Matthew 3:16–17). Christians synthesize these opposites whereas the Jewish faith does not. The Jewish faith maintains that God is One and can't be anything other than One. Christians believe that God is both One and Three simultaneously. The opposites are blended.

WHEN IS A PUZZLE NOT A PUZZLE?

The Bible has confusing puzzles, but it also has some truths that don't need solving. For example, Scripture states that all humans have sinned (Romans 3:23) and that the only way to God is through Jesus (John 14:6). Over and over in the Bible we find that Christ's death and resurrection are the basis for salvation (e.g., Titus 3:5–6). Although it's surprising that God loves us so much that He sent His own Son to die for us, there is no doubt that we enter a relationship with God through Jesus.

WHY SHOULD WE CARE?

Some Christians prefer not to deal with confusing puzzles. Perhaps their theology is "working" in their present circumstances. Maybe they don't have time. Or perhaps they fear generating the wrong answers or putting the pieces together the wrong way.

None of us wants to be wrong about our faith. We don't want to displease God. Trying to solve biblical puzzles seems risky. Yet we deal with risks every day that range from minor to major. We take a risk whenever we try a new breakfast cereal or a new bank. We learn to manage these risks. When we traveled to Asia, we managed the risk of malaria by taking anti-malaria medicine. Whenever we drive a car, we flirt with death. But we manage that risk by taking driving lessons, learning traffic laws and safety rules, taking a test to get a license, obeying traffic signs and signals, supporting law enforcement officials, and wearing our seatbelts. By managing the risk, most of us survive our daily brush with death.

THE ESSENCE OF GOD IS LOVE

God showed Himself to Moses by passing before him and introducing Himself as "The LORD, the LORD, the compassionate and gracious God, slow to anger, abounding in love and faithfulness, maintaining love to thousands, and forgiving wickedness, rebellion and sin. Yet he does not leave the guilty unpunished. . . ." (Exodus 34:6–7). We often repeat "For God so loved the world. . . ." (John 3:16) and "God is love" (1 John 4:16). We know that God is our Father who delights in giving us the desires of our heart (Psalm 37:4), good gifts (Matthew 7:11), and wisdom (James 1:5). We know that both the Holy Spirit (Romans 8:26–27) and Christ (Romans 8:34) are interceding for us. So does God suspend His love for us when we're stuck in one of life's puzzles? No! According to the apostle Paul,

> Who shall separate us from the love of Christ? Shall trouble or hardship or persecution or famine or nakedness or danger or sword? [Or feeling stuck?] . . . For I am convinced that neither death nor life, neither angels nor demons, neither the

> present nor the future, nor any powers,
> neither height nor depth, nor anything
> else in all creation [like feeling stuck in
> a life puzzle], will be able to separate us
> from the love of God that is in Christ Jesus
> our Lord." (Romans 8:35, 38–39)

We never eliminate the risk of being wrong, but we manage the risk by asking God for wisdom and by trusting our loving, all-knowing Father who cares deeply for our well-being.

QUESTIONS FOR GROUP DISCUSSION OR PERSONAL REFLECTION

- List some puzzles found in the Bible.

- Pick one of the Bible's puzzling truths and discuss possible solutions.

- Why do you think Jesus made puzzle-like statements?

- Which puzzles do you find most problematic? Why?

PUZZLE #1

MY PRIORITY

My Neighbor or Myself?

BLUE SKY

Others first

If someone strikes you on the right cheek, turn to him the other also. (Matthew 5:39)

GREEN TREE

Me first

"I appeal to Caesar!" – Paul (Acts 25:11)

COUNSELOR & CLIENT CONVERSATION

ME: Last week you were going to start to take care of
yourself instead of giving money to your brother. How
did that go?

CAROL: I bought him household items this week, but that was
all.

ME: So, you kind of followed your plan and kind of didn't.
What got in the way of following it all the way?

CAROL: I just don't think I can do something for me.

ME: Why not?

CAROL: I don't think God wants me to be selfish.

ME: What do you mean by "selfish"?

CAROL: Well, I think God wants me to love others.

ME: And not yourself?

CAROL: Right. I can't see how I can love myself without being
selfish.

ME: And you're worried about being selfish?

CAROL: Yes.

ME: Could it be that God wants you to take care of
yourself as well as your brother?

CAROL: No, it doesn't work that way.

ME: Why not?

CAROL: It's selfish to think about yourself.

ME: When God said to love your neighbor as yourself,
what does "as yourself" mean?

CAROL: I don't know. But I don't think it's possible to love
someone else and yourself at the same time.

CAROL STRUGGLED WITH HOW SHE COULD LOVE HER brother and herself. She didn't see how she could do what was good for herself without harming someone else. As a result, she concluded that she could either do what was good for others or what was good for her. She couldn't accomplish both.

To help her move through this stuck place, I encouraged her to see this struggle as a puzzle of blue sky and green tree pieces. God created her, loves her, and is committed to her well being in the same way that He created others, loves them, and is committed to their well being. It's not *either* others *or* her: it's *both* others *and* her.

Carol can love her brother *and* herself. To love herself is to honor the One who made her. She can help her brother financially without risking her own financial health, and she can set limits on when she'll be able to help him next. If he needs more help, she can give him the contact information for some food pantries.

WHAT IS SELFISHNESS?

When my husband went to pick up our oldest son from preschool, he saw him shove another child out of the way in his attempt to get out the door first. My husband explained that he should ask the child to move out of the way rather than shove him. Our son proceeded with a list of "what if" questions. What if he can't hear me? What if he won't listen? What if he still won't move?

We take great pains to teach our children how to behave in relationships with others. That's what Jesus was doing in His Sermon on the Mount. He taught that we're to turn the other cheek, give the person who is suing us our cloak, go the extra mile, and give to the person who wants to borrow from us (Matthew 5:38–42). As if that weren't enough, Jesus later told His followers to deny themselves and take up their cross and follow Him (Matthew 16:24).

Putting others first is not popular; putting ourselves first is. Common expressions focus on self: know yourself, be yourself, believe in yourself, express yourself, respect yourself, be honest with yourself, stand up for yourself, and even self-improvement.[2]

We value independence, not sharing. We have our own cars, phones, and TVs. We want what we want and we want it *now*. Fast Internet connections allow us to have online banking, online shopping, online chatting, and online news. We have on-demand movies. Our default setting is "self first."

UNSELFISH RUTH

The main character in the Old Testament book of Ruth had a different default setting. Ruth lived in Moab, and she was married to a Hebrew man who had moved there with his parents during a famine in Israel. His brother also married a Moabite girl. The brothers both died a short time after the death of their father, leaving their mother, Naomi, alone in a foreign country. When Naomi decided to return to her homeland, her daughter-in-law Ruth determined that she would take care of her mother-in-law even though it meant leaving her own home and country.

Naomi tried to convince Ruth to stay with her people because "the LORD's hand has gone out against me!" (Ruth 1:13). But Ruth would not be deterred. Though both were poor widows, Ruth had youth. She would be able to work and perhaps remarry. Naomi had little hope for a future. Without Ruth, it's hard to imagine how Naomi would have survived. Upon arriving in Israel, Ruth went out to glean in the fields. Naomi did not; perhaps she was too old. Ruth took her breadwinner duties seriously and went out every day to gather grain.

However, Ruth did more than glean food. She also asked the landowner, Boaz, to marry her! "Spread the corner of your garment over me," Ruth said to him (Ruth 3:9). The same statement was used by the prophet Ezekiel to refer to the solemn marriage covenant between God and Israel:

> "Later I passed by, and when I looked at you and saw that you were old enough for love, I spread the corner of my garment over you and covered your nakedness. I gave you my solemn oath and entered into a covenant with you, declares the Sovereign LORD, and you became mine." (Ezekiel 16:8)

Based on this comparison, Ruth almost certainly was proposing marriage.[3] She claimed her right to a kinsman-redeemer by proposing marriage to Boaz.

In Israel, kinsman-redeemers would help family or clan members in need. Ruth invited Boaz to fulfill his duty by marrying her. Boaz called Ruth an *eshet chayil*, or woman of strength. He admired Ruth not only because of her commitment to Naomi but also for her determination in asking for what she and Naomi needed: redemption.

DETERMINED RUTH

Ruth found a way to take care not only of herself but her mother-in-law as well. Instead of solving life's puzzle with a "me or others" approach, she solved it by taking care of both.

Ruth could have put herself first and simply found a young husband, as Boaz acknowledged: "You have not run after the younger men, whether rich or poor" (Ruth 3:10). But Ruth wanted a solution that worked for both her and Naomi. Her marriage to Boaz, their kinsman redeemer, solved both problems.

Side by side with Jesus' statements about turning the other cheek and denying ourselves, we find instances in which Jesus commended people for making known their requests. In fact, Jesus rewarded this type of assertiveness.

To the woman who touched the hem of His garment, Jesus said, "Daughter, your faith has healed you. Go in peace" (Luke 8:48). Impressed with the faith of the Syrophoenician woman who assertively pleaded her case, Jesus healed her daughter (Mark 7:30).

Yet we also find clear statements in the Bible about putting others first: "Be devoted to one another in . . . love. Honor one another above yourselves" (Romans 12:10).

Christians sometimes create unsolvable puzzles out

of these seemingly conflicting passages. Some Christians believe that we have to love ourselves first. Other Christians believe that we have to love others first. It's either-or. Either we love others *or* we love ourselves. But Jesus fit the puzzle pieces together: love others *as* you love yourselves (Matthew 22:39). We complete the puzzle by taking care of others *as* we take care of ourselves.

THE BLUE SKY PIECE: LOVING OTHERS

When our oldest son was three, he had a doll named Sally. Every event would generate the question, "What does Sally say about that?" If preschool was cancelled, he would ask, "What does Sally say about that?" I would dutifully answer, "She's kind of sad she won't see her friends today, but she's glad she gets to be at home." Sally's constant presence could get frustrating. One night at supper I finally said, "No Sally tonight! Dad and I are going to enjoy adult conversation." Our son said indignantly, "And what does Sally say about that!" His persistence in claiming front and center attention via Sally made me realize that people need attention.

Complete selflessness is a flawed solution to this life puzzle because it fails to acknowledge the fact that God created everyone with rights; we all have something to offer other than self-sacrifice.

RIGHTS

Those who live in the United States are guaranteed certain rights. The Declaration of Independence states:

> We hold these truths to be self-evident,
> that all men are created equal, that they
> are endowed by their Creator with
> certain unalienable Rights, that among
> these are Life, Liberty and the pursuit of
> Happiness.

The Bill of Rights elaborates, guaranteeing freedoms involving religion, speech, press, as well as the right not to be deprived of life, liberty, or property, without due process of law.

The Bible assumes that we have certain rights. In fact, the concept that people have rights and that all are created equal grows out of Judeo-Christian values and is based on the belief that each of us is created in the image of God (Genesis 1:7) and thus has God-given rights. Here are some of the rights that have a biblical basis:

- property (Exodus 22:1–15; Nehemiah 2:20)
- fair trial (Exodus 23:1–3, 6–9)
- inheritance (Deuteronomy 21:15–17)
- compensation for work (Leviticus 19:13)
- redemption rights (Ruth 4:4; Jeremiah 32:8)
- feeling our feelings and having our thoughts (Psalm 88)

We have the right to become a child of God (John 1:12), and to have our own convictions (Romans 14:5). However, we must be careful that the exercise of our rights "does not become a stumbling block to the weak" (1 Corinthians 8:9).

We see examples of Peter changing his mind (Acts

11:1–18), of Paul having ambition and goals (Romans 15:20), being assertive (Galatians 2:11–21), and setting limits in a relationship (Acts 15:36–40).

Paul mentioned certain rights of apostles:

> Don't we have the right to food and drink? Don't we have the right to take a believing wife along with us, as do the other apostles and the Lord's brothers and Cephas? Or is it only I and Barnabas who must work for a living? Who serves as a soldier at his own expense? Who plants a vineyard and does not eat of its grapes? Who tends a flock and does not drink of the milk? . . . If others have this right of support from you, shouldn't we have it all the more? But we did not use this right. On the contrary, we put up with anything rather than hinder the gospel of Christ. (1 Corinthians 9:4–7, 12)

Through the Old Testament prophets God pleaded with His people to respect the rights of those who couldn't claim their own rights—widows, orphans, and foreigners.

> If you really change your ways and your actions and deal with each other justly, if you do not oppress the alien, the fatherless or the widow and do not shed innocent blood in this place, and if you do not

follow other gods to your own harm, then
I will let you live in this place, in the land
I gave your forefathers for ever and ever.
(Jeremiah 7:5–7)

God told His people to care for the rights of widows;
He did not tell the orphans, widows, and foreigners to
give up their rights. His message was to the people who
had power; they were to make sure that the rights of the
powerless were respected. God cares about rights.

CLAIMING RIGHTS

Before our second son became a computer genius, he
deleted my mother's computer files. My mom is always
working on a book or a Bible study, so deleting the files was
not a good thing. Although she chose to forgive him, she
didn't let him near her computer without supervision after
that! She had the right to limit his access to her computer,
and she claimed that right. Even in the act of forgiveness
and forgoing retaliation, she had rights.

Jesus asserted His right as the Son of God to cleanse
the temple courtyard (John 2:12–16). He also recognized
the rights of government to collect taxes when He told the
Pharisees to give to Caesar what belongs to Caesar (Matthew
22:21). Paul appealed twice regarding his rights as a Roman
citizen (Acts 22:25; 25:11). He also respected other people's
rights, instructing believers to "give everyone what you owe
him: If you owe taxes, pay taxes; if revenue, then revenue; if
respect, then respect; if honor, then honor" (Romans 13:7).

Tamar was married to Judah's oldest son, but he died before they had children. According to Jewish law, she should have become the wife of the second son, Onan. However, Onan did not fulfill his duty and died because God was displeased with him. Judah should have made Tamar the wife of his younger son, Shelah, but instead he sent her back to her father's house. Tamar took the initiative to claim her right by pretending to be a prostitute and becoming pregnant by her father-in-law. When Judah realized what he had done, he acknowledged that she was entitled to claim her right: "She is more righteous than I, since I wouldn't give her to my son Shelah" (Genesis 38:26). "Righteousness" here refers to respecting rights; a righteous person respects rights. Justice recognizes that people have rights and upholds them.

Some Christians may worry that claiming our rights will put us on God's blacklist, but Tamar ended up in Matthew's genealogy of Jesus (Matthew 1:3).

God Himself is concerned about our rights. Micah was confident that God would uphold his right. "Because I have sinned against him, I will bear the LORD's wrath, until he pleads my case and establishes my right" (Micah 7:9). God upholds our rights because He "loves justice" (Psalm 11:7). "For you have upheld my right and my cause; you have sat on your throne, judging righteously" (Psalm 9:4).

God upholds our rights, and He wants us to uphold the rights of others, especially the rights of those who can't help themselves. "Speak up for those who cannot speak for themselves, for the rights of all who are destitute. Speak up and judge fairly; defend the rights of the poor and needy"

(Proverbs 31:8–9). Failing to uphold someone else's rights is reprehensible to God. "To deny a man his rights before the Most High, to deprive a man of justice—would not the LORD see such things?" (Lamentations 3:35–36).

GIVING UP RIGHTS

In addition to having rights, we also have the right to give them up. Jesus said, "You have heard that it was said, 'Eye for eye, and tooth for tooth.' But I tell you . . . If someone strikes you on the right cheek, turn to him the other also" (Matthew 5:38–39). In this statement, Jesus gave us the right to give up our rights to retaliation. We have the right to solve our problems with our enemies and get our relationships right with them.

Bishop Desmond Tutu, who worked with the Truth and Reconciliation Commission of South Africa to develop a reconciliation plan to bring together the whites who had abused the rights of blacks during apartheid, wrote:

> If we are going to move on and build a new kind of world community there must be a way in which we can deal with a sordid past. The most effective way would be for the perpetrators or their descendants to acknowledge the awfulness of what happened and the descendants of the victims to respond by granting forgiveness, providing something can be done, even symbolically, to compensate for the

> anguish experienced, whose consequences
> are still being lived through today. . . . true
> forgiveness deals with the past, all of the
> past, to make the future possible.[4]

Even in the process of forgiveness and reconciliation, we retain our right for "something to be done."

God sent three years of famine on Israel because they had outrageously disregarded the Gibeonites' right to life during the reign of Saul (2 Samuel 21). King David asked them: "how shall I make amends?" (v. 3). They claimed their right, and David had seven male descendants of Saul killed (v. 6).

Even God does not give up His right for "something to be done." He required atonement or reparation for our sin. The truly unexpected piece of the story is that God Himself in His Son paid all the reparations for the injuries that our sin caused. Jesus' atonement is the basis for our reconciliation with God. It was God's right to request atonement: "without the shedding of blood there is no forgiveness" (Hebrews 9:22). He claimed the right for "something to be done." He claimed it and He fulfilled it. God worked relentlessly to repair His relationship with us, even though He was the injured party. God models for us how to work toward reconciliation instead of revenge.

When a group from work went skiing, I paid for a coworker's lift ticket. I didn't know him well, but whenever I would see him, I'd remind him he still owed me money. I was annoyed that he didn't repay me. Finally, I realized that he didn't intend to pay me back. I suspect that it was a hardship for him. I could have demanded payment. I knew his supervisor, and I could have made trouble for him. But I finally decided that I would forgive his debt. I didn't want to have that nagging at the back of my mind anymore. So I willfully incurred the cost of his ski ticket so that I could be at peace with him. I didn't claim the right to get paid back. I had that right, but I gave it up so that our relationship could be right. At times, we do that. This is a paltry example of what Jesus did on the cross for us. We couldn't pay the price. So He did. God turned the other cheek.

DON'T RETALIATE!

The film *Munich*, directed by Steven Spielberg, tells the story of what happened after eleven Israeli athletes were massacred during the 1972 Olympic Games in Munich. Israel's government sent an undercover team of assassins to get revenge. The film debates the value of revenge because the only result is more revenge. The film asks, where does it end? Jesus has an answer: it ends when one party turns the other cheek.

Jesus made the important point that turning the other cheek gets a better result than retaliation: "You have heard that it was said, 'Eye for eye, and tooth for tooth.' But I tell you, Do not resist an evil person. If someone strikes you on the right cheek, turn to him the other also" (Matthew 5:38–39). Find a way to resolve the conflict without letting it spiral into revenge.

We no longer have to give as good as we get. Jesus affirmed the proverb: "A man's wisdom gives him patience;

it is to his glory to overlook an offense" (19:11). Working through conflict is the best course of action as we forgive "our debtors" (Matthew 6:12). The passage emphasizes that "if you forgive men when they sin against you, your heavenly Father will also forgive you. But if you do not forgive men their sins, your Father will not forgive your sins" (Matthew 6:14–15). The exhortation of the Sermon on the Mount is to work through conflicts and forgive because revenge doesn't achieve anything but more revenge. Mohandas Gandhi put it this way: "An eye for eye only ends up making the whole world blind."

SELF-DENIAL

We can claim rights and we can give them up, but what about denying ourselves? Jesus said, "If anyone would come after me, he must deny himself and take up his cross and follow me" (Matthew 16:24). This seems to indicate that we are to love others above ourselves. But consider the context. Jesus was preparing for His death. He explained to His disciples that He must die (Matthew 16:21). Peter rebuked Him: "Never, Lord! This shall never happen to you!" (v. 22). Jesus answered, "Get behind me, Satan! You are a stumbling block to me; you do not have in mind the things of God, but the things of men" (v. 23). It was during this discussion that Jesus said His disciples must deny themselves. In other words, disciples must be willing to die. He continued, "For whoever wants to save his life will lose it, but whoever loses his life for me will find it" (v. 25). Denying oneself is not a statement about never claiming rights or not taking care of oneself. It's a statement about counting the cost of discipleship. Jesus is saying that whoever follows Him should be ready for anything, even death. It's like the adolescent experience of associating with the "wrong person"; it's the kiss of death to popularity. Association with Jesus bears with it certain liabilities, one of which could be a literal or figurative "kiss of death."

If Matthew 16:24 is not a statement about self-denial, surely Philippians 2:3–5 is. In this passage, Paul said that we are to "consider others better than yourselves. Each of you should look not only to your own interests, but also to the interests of others. Your attitude should be the same as that of Christ Jesus."

This seems to indicate that we should take care of others and not ourselves. But Paul's statements in Philippians 2:3 are similar to the words of Jesus when He said, "Love your neighbor as yourself" (Matthew 22:39). Paul told Christians to "look not only to your own interests, but also to the interests of others." Jesus said that the Law and the Prophets can be summed up in this statement: "In everything, do to others what you would have them do to you" (Matthew 7:12). Jesus was setting up reciprocity, not zero or negative attention on ourselves. As Melody Beattie noted in *Codependent No More*, we wouldn't dream of treating other people the way we treat ourselves (or let ourselves be treated).[5]

C. S. Lewis wrote: "Christian renunciation does not mean stoic 'apathy,' but a readiness to prefer God to inferior ends which are in themselves lawful" (*The Problem of Pain*).

TAKE CARE OF YOURSELF SO YOU CAN TAKE CARE OF OTHERS

How is this done? Human nature is limited. Our needs sometimes compete with those of other people.

I love to be at home, and my husband loves to be out and about. How can we reconcile these opposite needs? If I always honor his need to be out and about, I will quickly become exhausted and won't have any energy left to give to him. But by taking care of my own need for solitude, I ultimately take care of his need to be out and about. By taking care of ourselves, we are able to take care of others. The airline instructions are clear: we put on our own oxygen mask before trying to help someone else. Why? Because we can't help others if we're not breathing!

Am I selfishly sinning when I take care of myself? No. In fact, one God-given way we care for ourselves is by taking Sabbath rests. God Himself rested after completing the work of creation (Genesis 2:2–3; Exodus 20:8–11). Jesus told His disciples to rest because they hadn't had a chance to eat. He said, "Come with me by yourselves to a quiet place and get some rest" (Mark 6:31).

THE GREEN TREE PIECE: TAKING CARE OF MYSELF

Some Christians have no problem taking care of themselves. Instead, they wonder why they should have to take care of others. Loving others—what's in it for me?

But anyone who wants to be a Christian must love others. You can't be a Christian without loving others. We love others because God loves us *and* them.

> If anyone says, "I love God," yet hates
> his brother, he is a liar. For anyone who
> does not love his brother, whom he has
> seen, cannot love God, whom he has not
> seen. And he has given us this command:
> Whoever loves God must also love his
> brother. (1 John 4:20–21)

If you're unsure about your Christian duty to love others, read all of 1 John or 1 Corinthians 13:1–3, which speaks of the high calling of love:

> If I speak in the tongues of men and of
> angels, but have not love, I am only a
> resounding gong or a clanging cymbal. If I
> have the gift of prophecy and can fathom
> all mysteries and all knowledge, and if I
> have a faith that can move mountains, but
> have not love, I am nothing. If I give all
> I possess to the poor and surrender my
> body to the flames, but have not love, I
> gain nothing. (1 Corinthians 13:1–3)

Jesus told His disciples that love is the defining characteristic of His followers: "By this all men will know that you are my disciples, if you love one another" (John 13:35). The love He talked about isn't mushy feelings. It's a willingness to follow Him to the point of death. "My command is this: Love each other as I have loved you. Greater love has no one than this: that he lay down his life for his friends" (John 15:12–13). We put ourselves out for others, even to the point of death. "Be imitators of God, therefore, as dearly loved children and live a life of love, just as Christ loved us and gave himself up for us as a fragrant offering and sacrifice to God" (Ephesians 5:1–2).

This love extends not only to people we like, but also to those we don't. When Jesus told the Parable of the Good Samaritan, He made clear that we are to show love to everyone, even the unlovable (Luke 10:37). Do we have to put ourselves out for others? Yes. We inconvenience ourselves as much as Jesus did when He died for us. Death is the quintessential example of putting yourself out for others. Paul said,

> Do nothing out of selfish ambition or vain conceit, but in humility consider others better than yourselves. Each of you should look not only to your own interests but also to the interests of others. (Philippians 2:3–4).

We put ourselves out for others by being compassionate, kind, humble, gentle, patient, and forgiving.

> Therefore, as God's chosen people, holy and dearly loved, clothe yourselves with compassion, kindness, humility, gentleness and patience. Bear with each other and forgive whatever grievances you may have against one another. Forgive as the Lord

forgave you. And over all these virtues put
on love, which binds them all together in
perfect unity. (Colossians 3:12–14)

The Bible has an unmistakable green tree piece: we are
to love others.

HOW DO WE LOVE OTHERS AND OURSELVES?

How do we do both? In *The Purpose-Driven Life,* Rick
Warren says, "Service to others is thinking of ourselves less,
but not thinking less of ourselves." We think of our needs
and also consider the needs of others.

A family moving to Denver called us late on a Friday
afternoon and asked to stay at our house. They were almost
strangers. They knew some friends of some friends of
ours. We were tenth on their contact list, so nine others
had refused to shelter them for one reason or another. The
others chose to claim their right *not* to share their space.
We all had that right. I wanted to refuse as well, but we
agreed to let them stay for four days, long enough for them
to find a more permanent place. We chose to give up our
right to privacy, but only for four days. Others might have
let them live with them for the next four months, but we
limited their stay to four days. Why? Because I have the
right to do that in my own house. I can tolerate company
for short periods of time; I don't want to let people stay so
long that I resent their presence. I don't like being a hostage
to other people's undefined timelines; their emergency isn't
necessarily mine. However, I am willing to put myself

out for a few days. They had young children, and I had what they needed—a place to stay. "If anyone has material possessions and sees his brother in need but has no pity on him, how can the love of God be in him?" (1 John 3:17). We found a solution that worked for both of us.

FINDING WIN-WIN SOLUTIONS

Many problems have win-win solutions[6] even when there doesn't appear to be one. The family moving to Denver wanted to be our guests; we wanted privacy. With those stated goals, it would be hard to come up with a win-win solution. The mutually exclusive goals are win-lose. Someone wins and someone loses.

The best way to generate win-win solutions is to look at underlying interests and find a way to bring them together. The family moving to Denver was interested in finding a safe place for their children. We were interested in maintaining order in our home. A win-win solution involved giving them a safe place for a limited amount of time.

Some win-win solutions are hard to find simply because people aren't interested in finding them. But win-win solutions allow us to love others *and* ourselves. They enable us to put the two puzzle pieces together, the blue sky piece of loving others and the green tree piece of loving ourselves. Alone, neither completes the puzzle. We love others and ourselves at all times.

QUESTIONS FOR GROUP DISCUSSION OR PERSONAL REFLECTION

■ List some of your rights.

■ Describe a situation when you claimed a right and a situation when you chose to give up a right.

■ How do you feel when you claim a right?

■ How do you feel when you choose to give up a right?

■ How do you know when to claim a right and when to give it up?

MY CONDITION

Woefully Sinful or Wonderfully Made?

BLUE SKY

My guilt has overwhelmed me like a burden too heavy to bear. (Psalm 38:4)

For I know my transgressions, and my sin is always before me.

Surely I was sinful at birth, sinful from the time my mother conceived me. (Psalm 51:3, 5)

GREEN TREE

I praise you because I am fearfully and wonderfully made; your works are wonderful, I know that full well. (Psalm 139:14)

This is what the LORD says—your Redeemer, who formed you in the womb:

I am the LORD, who has made all things, who alone stretched out the heavens, who spread out the earth by myself. (Isaiah 44:24)

COUNSELOR & CLIENT CONVERSATION

ME: So, doing something for yourself is selfish?

CAROL: Yes; it's not right to do something for me.

ME: Why not?

CAROL: For a lot of reasons, but partly because I'm sinful.

ME: So being sinful means that you can't take care of yourself?

CAROL: That's right. Sinful people have to pay for their sinfulness.

ME: But aren't people also wonderfully made by God?

CAROL: They might be wonderfully made but sin kind of trumps that.

As man's insight increases so he finds both wretchedness and greatness within himself. In a word man knows he is wretched. Thus he is wretched because he is so, but he is truly great because he knows it. (Blaise Pascal, *Pensées*)

THE BIBLE HAS MANY REFERENCES TO THE "SINFUL nature" (e.g., Romans 7–8; Galatians 5), and it states in no uncertain terms that "If we claim to be without sin, we deceive ourselves" (1 John 1:8). We have examples in the Bible of people who sin repeatedly (e.g., Samson, Abraham, and the people of Israel). And we can see sin in our own lives when we speak unkindly, covet, envy, steal, or lie. Most of us agree that we struggle daily with sin. The blue sky piece of our sinful nature is indisputable. In his hymn "Amazing Grace," songwriter John Newton referred to himself as a "wretch."

Growing up, I pictured the "sinful nature" as a villain in a cartoon—a short man with a thin handlebar moustache, shifty eyes, dressed in black and wearing a stovepipe hat—always lurking in the background waiting to trip me up.

WONDERFULLY MADE

However, the psalmist lays out a green tree piece. We are "fearfully and wonderfully made" (Psalm 139:14). We have amazing capabilities, and we live with a nature poisoned by sin. We need to understand both aspects. Understanding our sinfulness and our wonderfulness allows us to enter into a relationship with God, with ourselves, and with others. This understanding allows us to complete this life puzzle.

The man who wrote about being "fearfully and wonderfully made" embodied the best and worst of humanity. At a desperate time in Israel's history, David gained victory over the Philistines (1 Samuel 17). But later in his life he ordered a man killed to cover up his own adultery with the man's wife (2 Samuel 11). Yet David was a "man after God's own heart" (1 Samuel 13:14; Acts 13:22). Sin and splendor wrapped into one package.

WONDERFUL HUMAN BIOLOGY

Our bodies are composed of trillions of atoms that have been around since the creation of the universe. It takes about 22 muscles working together to smile.[7] While you read this page, hundreds of chemical reactions are taking place in your eyes.[8] Your brain has approximately 100 billion neurons.[9] Your nose helps you to taste.[10] The DNA code in each of our cells could fill 300,000 pages if written as letters. In fact, the DNA in all of the more than 100 trillion cells in our body could stretch to the sun and back 500 times! We are truly wonderfully made. Isaac Newton has been quoted as saying, "In the absence of any other proof, the thumb alone would convince me of God's existence."[11]

WONDERFUL IMAGE BEARERS

We are especially wonderful because we are image bearers of God: "So God created man in his own image, in the image of God he created him; male and female he created them" (Genesis 1:27). Even after the fall we bear His image. "Whoever sheds the blood of man, by man shall his blood be shed; for in the image of God has God made man" (Genesis 9:6). The Hebrew word for image (zelem) means "representation" or "likeness." The word was used for the statue of a king who had conquered enemy territory. We are the representation of God as He is infiltrating Satan's realm, the earth, by spreading His people throughout the kingdom. If you want to see what God is like, look at His people.

WONDERFUL HOLY PEOPLE

Scripture refers to God's people as holy. "But you are a chosen people, a royal priesthood, a holy nation, a people belonging to God, that you may declare the praises of him who called you out of darkness into his wonderful light" (1 Peter 2:9). In Peter's day, the word *holy* meant "no longer common." We have passed into the realm of the sacred. We are "special."

WONDERFUL UNIQUE PEOPLE

Look at all the people around you—neighbors, co-workers, commuters, people at church—and notice how different we are. Not only do we all look different, we all behave differently. We have different interests. We think different thoughts. We value different things.

People are unique in physical traits—like having freckles, blond hair, dimples, or being tall—or in character traits—like being quiet, organized, opinionated, or helpful. Traits are innumerable and can be combined in countless ways. Each trait exists on a spectrum—from a little to a lot of it. Which traits a person has, and how much of it, forms each person's unique personality.

I am average in height and weight. I'm not a pack rat or a neat-nick! I am very near sighted. I'm more frugal than most people. I love adventure more than most people. I have low blood pressure. I eat fewer sweets than most Americans. I don't like to change my mind as much as others do. These traits just scratch the surface of my identity.

In the book of Exodus, we meet a person named Moses who spent his early years with his Hebrew family in Egypt and then several years in a royal Egyptian household as the adopted son of Pharaoh's daughter. "Moses was educated in all the wisdom of the Egyptians and was powerful in speech and action" (Acts 7:22). Despite living in Pharaoh's household, Moses maintained his loyalty to the Hebrews. This loyalty combined with sensitivity to injustice got Moses in trouble. He killed an Egyptian who was mistreating a Hebrew slave and then fled to Midian, where he spent the next forty years in the desert (Acts 7:29–30). In Midian, Moses continues to show his sensitivity to injustice. A priest of Midian had seven daughters who came to draw water for their father's flock. Some shepherds came along and drove them away, but Moses came to their rescue (see Exodus 2:15–17). He was sensitive to others.

Moses also was an arguer. He argued with God several times (Exodus 5:12, 22–23) and God listened. Moses seems to have been conversant in several cultures and languages. Even though he was reluctant to talk to Pharaoh, and mentions his slow speech to God several times (Exodus 4:10; 6:12, 30), he was nonetheless a gifted arguer, probably in several languages.

After God created Moses, he placed him in situations

where he developed connections to Pharaoh's court. In Midian, Moses developed the skills to negotiate desert life. God made sure when he created Moses that he would be uniquely positioned with the traits (personality, skills, and connections) to accomplish what God needed. More important than any trait, Moses was friends with God: "The LORD would speak to Moses face to face, as a man speaks with his friend" (Exodus 33:11). Moses argued with God, prayed to God, even asked God to show Himself to him. And God did (Exodus 34:5–7).

We can see God's creative work in David as well. David was distinctive physically. The Bible describes him as "ruddy, with a fine appearance and handsome features" (1 Samuel 16:12). But he was also distinctive in personality. His oldest brother, Eliab, found David annoying and called him "conceited" (1 Samuel 17:28).

However, David had a lot going for him. He was an accomplished musician who was selected to play for the king (1 Samuel 16:18)—and thereby had the opportunity to observe firsthand how to be king. He was a gifted poet who wrote songs that beautifully capture the ups and downs of his unique relationship with God. David threw himself wholeheartedly into whatever he did: killing giants (1 Samuel 17); being friends with Jonathan (1 Samuel 20:41–42); being faithful to that friendship (2 Samuel 9:7); being a successful warrior and strategist (1 Samuel 18:5–7); acting crazy to save his life (1 Samuel 21:13); enthusiastically dancing before the LORD (2 Samuel 6:14); and not backing down in front of his wife (2 Samuel 6:21–22).

God created David with the traits of bravery and

enthusiasm. He created a man who could see the big picture and devise war strategies, who had the strength to wield weapons of war, who valued friendship with people and God, who made others want to follow him, and who had the ambition to take the territory that God had promised to Israel. All of these characteristics were critical to his role as king.

In the New Testament we meet Paul, a man "thoroughly trained in the law" under Gamaliel (Acts 22:3), one of the most honored teachers of first-century Israel. Under Gamaliel, Paul learned how to argue Jewish theology. Following his conversion, Paul used that skill in his preaching and writing. What perfect preparation for preaching in the marketplace of Athens (Acts 17), and to the Roman governors Felix (Acts 24) and Festus (Acts 25), and to King Agrippa (Acts 26). What perfect preparation for writing the epistles.

Apparently, Paul was a better writer than speaker. Face to face, Paul could be timid, but in his writing he was bold (2 Corinthians 10:1). Some Corinthians said, "his letters are weighty and forceful, but in person he is unimpressive and his speaking amounts to nothing" (v. 10). Paul admitted he was not a trained speaker (2 Corinthians 11:6). But he wrote to the Romans, "It has always been my ambition to preach the gospel where Christ was not known, so that I would not be building on someone else's foundation" (Romans 15:20). He apparently appreciated the challenge of preaching where no one had preached before.

Paul worked hard so that he would not have to rely on new converts to support him (v. 23). He worked out of a sense of integrity and fairness to others. He wrote to the Thessalonians:

> We were not idle when we were with you, nor did we eat anyone's food without paying for it. On the contrary, we worked night and day, laboring and toiling so that we would not be a burden to any of you. We did this, not because we do not have the right to such help, but in order to make ourselves a model for you to follow. For even when we were with you, we gave you this rule: "if a man will not work, he shall not eat." (2 Thessalonians 3:7–10)

Paul also was a man of strong conviction, evidenced first when he was persecuting Christians and later when he persevered through severe persecution for his faith in Christ.

Following his conversion, Paul never gave up his faith despite being severely beaten and imprisoned several times (Acts 16:22–23). In fact, Paul says that he was "in prison more frequently, been flogged more severely, and been exposed to death" (2 Corinthians 11:23) more than other apostles. When God created him, He made sure he had the traits necessary for the work ahead of him.

God's intent in His creation of Moses, David, and Paul is easy to see. But was God as intentional when He created each of us?

God has innumerable choices when He creates each

person. Some choices—like gender, race, height, and weight—are obvious. But some are not. Think about your own talents and abilities as well as those of the people you know. For example, the ability to build, cook, guide a child, teach a class, respond to an emergency, play the piano, administer, manage, lead, analyze, budget, perform, coordinate, schedule, decide, create, design, explain, fundraise, argue, conceptualize, organize, delegate, coach, pack, assemble, proofread, sell, compose, arrange. And these are just a sample. The list is huge.

If you take all the traits listed above, and consider that all those traits exist in individuals on a spectrum, and add in the possible combinations, the number of types of people are endless. God created amazing individuality and uniqueness in all people. People are intricate and unique works of art. No two are alike. The wonder of our amazing creation is indisputable.

In *The Problem of Pain*, C. S. Lewis wrote:

> If He had no use for all these differences, I do not see why He should have created more souls than one. Be sure that the ins and outs of your individuality are no mystery to Him; and one day they will no longer be a mystery to you. The mould in which a key is made would be a strange thing, if you had never seen a key: and the key itself a strange thing if you had never seen a lock. Your soul has a curious shape because it is a hollow made to fit a

particular swelling the infinite contours of the divine substance, or a key to unlock one of the doors in the house with many mansions. . . . Each of the redeemed shall forever know and praise some one aspect of the divine beauty better than any other creature can. Why else were individuals created, but that God, loving all infinitely, should love each differently. . . . If all experienced God in the same way and returned Him an identical worship, the song of the Church triumphant would have no symphony, it would be like an orchestra in which all the instruments played the same note. (pp. 147, 150)

SINFUL NATURE

On the other hand, the Bible has a lot to say about our sinful nature. Having gotten the impression early in my life that the Bible was full of heroes of the faith, I was shocked by what I found when I started reading Scripture for myself: murder, rape, pillage, infidelity, treachery, unjust imprisonment, and violent retaliation, to list just a few! If we're so wonderfully made, how can we also be so sinful?

As much as some would like to explain away sin, its record in the Bible and its evidence in the world is impossible to dismiss: war, murder, adultery, infidelity, stealing, lies, bitterness, gossip, hatred, fits of rage. It's equally hard to ignore the evidence of sin in us: lying "a little," taking something that doesn't belong to us, fantasizing about sex with someone we're not married to. We have to face the fact that "we all have sinned" (Romans 3:23).

Dr. Gordon Lewis, one of my seminary professors, often said that we all have a sinful nature and we all confirm our sinful nature by choosing to sin. Milton Erickson wrote: "It is not simply that we are sinners because we sin; we sin because we are sinners."[12] As much as I don't like being reminded of my sin, "we" includes me. I want to be perfect, but I'm not. I want to be accepted by God for the good that I do, but I have nothing to offer.

In my more lucid moments, I admit that my natural impulse is to be bitter, to gossip, to hate, to let anger turn into rage. I try to guard against these impulses, but having to do so provides yet more evidence of my inherent sinfulness. The issue is not how I "manage" my sinfulness, but that I am sinful. Those who refuse to admit their sinfulness have little reason to acknowledge their need for a Savior.[13] Sin is the bad news; God's love and the salvation we have in Jesus is the good news. And although I am a sinner, I am a sinner who bears God's image and the stamp of His imagination.

David was an exceptional man by anyone's standards, and he was also a sinful man. After the prophet Nathan confronted him with his sins of adultery and murder, David wrote this moving confession:

> Have mercy on me, O God, according to
> your unfailing love; according to your great

compassion blot out my transgressions. Wash away all my iniquity and cleanse me from my sin. For I know my transgressions, and my sin is always before me. Against you, you only, have I sinned and done what is evil in your sight, so that you are proved right when you speak and justified when you judge. Surely I was sinful at birth, sinful from the time my mother conceived me. Surely you desire truth in the inner parts; you teach me wisdom in the inmost place. Cleanse me with hyssop, and I will be clean; wash me, and I will be whiter than snow. (Psalm 51:1-7)

David accepted his sinful nature (v. 5) and at the same time had confidence in God's love and forgiveness. He affirms that he will be clean (v. 7); he will be whiter than snow because God will forgive him. David had an unshakable confidence in God's desire to forgive him and to have a relationship with him. Sin wasn't enough to keep God away from David, and it's not enough to keep God away from you. God loves you despite your sin. Why? A part of the answer lies in your being created in His image and being one of His unique creations. Just as God created David uniquely, He has created you: a unique work of beauty, loved by Him.

Like blue sky and green tree pieces of a puzzle, all humans are a mixture of sin and beauty. Moses and Paul were unique men, but they had to deal with their sin. When

Moses pleaded with God to "forgive our wickedness and our sin, and take us as your inheritance," he acknowledged his own sin and need for forgiveness. Before his conversion, the apostle Paul dragged Christians off to prison (Acts 8:3) and made murderous threats against them (Acts 9:1). He referred to his own sin as well as ours when he wrote, "There is now no condemnation for those who are in Christ Jesus" (Romans 8:1).

We are unique people with sinful natures, and God can forgive us.

Terrorists held Martin and Gracia Burnham for over a year in the jungles of the Philippines. One day, Martin said to his wife, "Here in the mountains I've seen hatred; I've seen bitterness; I've seen greed; I've seen covetousness; I've seen wrong-doing." Gracia agreed with Martin. But Martin surprised Gracia when he said he hadn't been talking about the Abu Sayyaf terrorists. "I've seen each of these things in myself," he said. "The Lord has been showing me how incredibly sinful I am."[14] Martin was a calm, optimistic man who persevered under some of the most challenging circumstances, giving encouragement to his wife and other captives, remaining devoted to his God to the end. He was sinful and yet wonderfully made.

When we think of ourselves, do we pay more attention to our sinful nature or our unique beauty? Both the blue sky piece of our sinfulness and the green tree piece of our amazing nature belong side by side in this puzzle.

QUESTIONS FOR GROUP DISCUSSION OR PERSONAL REFLECTION

- List some of the positive qualities God created in you.

- What are some of your most unique characteristics?

- What might keep you from valuing your positive qualities?

- What might cause you to deny your sin?

- How do you manage to value yourself as a sinful person?

- How do you think God manages to love sinful creations?

GOD'S LOVE
Gift or Reward?

BLUE SKY

For God did not send his Son into the world to condemn the world, but to save the world through him. (John 3:17)

While we were still sinners, Christ died for us. (Romans 5:8)

GREEN TREE

Faith without deeds is dead. (James 2:26)

Continue to work out your salvation with fear and trembling. (Philippians 2:12)

COUNSELOR & CLIENT CONVERSATION

ME: So it's hard for you to accept God's love because you find it hard to believe that God can love someone sinful so freely?

CAROL: Yes, I'm trying not to be too sinful. I just want to even the score a bit. There is no free lunch and I don't believe salvation is really free.

ME: If it's not free, what does it cost?

CAROL: Well, it costs me being a good person. But I just keep messing up. I've worked hard to stop lying, but I just can help myself. I just fall back into all my old habits.

ME: And you think that's a problem for God?

CAROL: Of course. He wants me to be a good human being; I just can't seem to swing it.

ME: So what happens when you try and try and you keep failing?

CAROL: I'm sick of being a failure. I just want to give up.

ME: So, God wants you to be a good human being and you keep working to be good, but you're not successful and you want to give up?

CAROL: Yeah. I'm working hard for God to love me but I don't think He ever will. I'm just not good enough.

ME: So you can't accept God's love, you want to work for it?

CAROL: I'm trying to!

FOR AGES, HUMANS HAVE BEEN TRYING TO COVER up their imperfections by striving for perfection. The Greeks tried to create perfect buildings and statues, the Pharisees in the time of Jesus tried to follow God's law perfectly, and Leonardo Da Vinci tried to capture a perfect smile on the Mona Lisa. Civilizations fascinated by perfection are populated with citizens who strive to hide their humanity and sinfulness.

Humans are attracted to perfection like moths to a deadly flame. In fact, many people are far more interested in human perfection than God is. We read Jesus' words, "Be perfect, therefore, as your heavenly Father is perfect" (Matthew 5:48), and we falsely assume that "perfect" means perfectly following a set of dos and don'ts.

The Pharisees in Jesus' time thought that if they could perfectly follow a set of very complex laws, God would approve of them. But Jesus made the point that such perfection is the wrong goal.

Jesus began His argument at the beginning of the Sermon on the Mount (Matthew 5:1) when He said, "Unless your righteousness surpasses that of the Pharisees and the teachers of the law, you will certainly not enter the kingdom of heaven" (Matthew 5:20). Jesus then contrasted six teachings of the Pharisees with God's teaching. He essentially said, "Don't be perfect like the Pharisees. Be perfect like God."

God's perfection isn't a set of dos and don'ts. God's perfection is about loving people. When we assume that God needs us to be perfect, or to behave perfectly according to a set of rules so that He can love us, we misunderstand this passage. It is telling us that when we love God, we will love people. When we really love God, we won't try to earn His love by trying to be perfect.

THE PUZZLE PIECES OF PERFECTIONISM AND IMPERFECTION

Even if I could quote all of the verses about God's love for us (and I can't because there are so many), we might still wonder how God can love imperfect people. We might think that God cares about our perfection and that we must work hard to be perfect. We try never to lose keys or tempers; we try to remember our appointments and try not to make stupid suggestions in staff meetings. We want to offer God something. We hold onto our belief that there must be *something* we can bring to the relationship. We've been taught to pull our weight. We don't want to show up to dinner without bringing the dessert. We don't want to sit on the couch and watch someone else do all the work while we do nothing. We don't want to freeload off someone else's good graces. But this is one time when we're supposed to do just that. As Paul wrote to the Ephesians: "It is by grace you have been saved, through faith—and this not from yourselves, it is the gift of God—not by works, so that no one can boast" (Ephesians 2:8–9).

We can't boast because we contribute nothing. If we try to bring anything, even something small, to God as a basis for our relationship with Him, we are attempting to earn our salvation. But since salvation is by grace, "it is no longer by works; if it were, grace would no longer be grace" (Romans 11:6).

We try to put together our life puzzle with the green tree piece of perfection and the blue sky piece of imperfection, but they do not fit together, so God offers an entirely new set of puzzle pieces: God's grace. Paul thanks God for these different pieces. "Thanks be to God—through Jesus Christ our Lord!" (Romans 7:25).

As sinners, we have no spiritual currency to purchase our redemption. It had to be purchased by Christ, the righteous one. The assumptions that God wants our perfection and that we can achieve perfection are just plain false.

After my husband had a particularly hard week at work, I decided to give him a Saturday by himself to regroup. I took the kids and headed to my parents' house to give him time alone. But time alone wasn't what he needed; he needed to have us around. I assumed, since I like to be by myself to regroup, that he did too. I was determined to give him what I would have needed.

Sometimes we misunderstand God the way I misunderstood my husband. We insist on giving Him something He doesn't want.

WHAT DOES GOD WANT?

God relates to us on the basis of Christ's perfection, not ours. We have no righteousness of our own, so we have to rely on the righteousness of Jesus (see Romans 10:4).

God looks at Jesus' righteousness, not our own, because God knows we are sinful and incapable of producing righteousness. Just as we don't expect a chocolate cake mix to produce a lemon meringue pie, God doesn't expect us to produce perfection. We rely on Christ's perfection, and we work out our salvation, but how?

TWO TYPES OF IMPERFECTION

Humans are saddled with two types of imperfection: innate sinfulness and human limitations. I once worked for a very critical boss. When I left the job, I let some people know what kind of boss she had been. One of my motivations was to make sure that others wouldn't have to suffer as I had, but another motivation was revenge. I wanted her to hurt as much as I had been hurt. That was my sinful nature at work. I need Jesus' righteousness because of my sinful nature.

The other kind of imperfection has to do with such things as being limited by space and time, not knowing the future, making inevitable mistakes, and not being able to remember every piece of information.

My friend Jan once asked me for my recipe for yeast rolls. I told her that the recipe was a "sure thing." "You can't make a mistake with it," I assured her. But I forgot to tell her not to put hot water on yeast or it will die. When her rolls didn't rise, I remembered (too late) that I forgot to tell her about the hot water rule. Her rolls didn't rise because of my imperfection.

My husband and I are notorious for thinking we're talking about the same thing when we're not. Once (before cell phones) we were going to meet at McDonald's for lunch; I waited at one McDonald's for an hour while he was at another McDonald's a few miles away.

God is aware of these limitations. As the psalmist wrote, God "knows how we are formed, He remembers that we are dust" (Psalm 103:14). After creating Adam and Eve, God gave them an enthusiastic two thumbs up. Despite their limitations, God looked at them and described His work as "very good" (Genesis 1:31).

God also knows that we are sinners: "The eyes of the LORD are everywhere, keeping watch on the wicked and the good" (Proverbs 15:3). God knows that we struggle with sin. But despite our sin He loves us to death—His own death: "While we were still sinners, Christ died for us" (Romans 5:8).

When we invite people to our home, we clean the house to make our visitors believe this is how we always live. We would be embarrassed to have people know how we really live. Sometimes we do the same with God. We know our lives are not clean enough for God, so we don't want to invite Him in. We think we can hide the chaos of our lives from Him. This is obviously ridiculous. Once we accept our sinful nature, we no longer need to hide from God and can then accept His free gift of salvation. The important piece of perfection in the universe is Jesus' perfect sacrifice on the cross.

EVIDENCE OF PERFECTIONISM

Lies are an indication of our perfectionism because we use them to hide our imperfection. I once dropped a friend's painting that I had picked up to admire. I didn't want to admit what I had done, so I thought about coming up with some other explanation as to why the painting was now a little scuffed.

The Bible records many instances of lying. While Moses was on Mount Sinai getting the Ten Commandments from God, Aaron and the people of Israel got tired of waiting for him. In Exodus 32:2, Aaron said to the people of Israel that they should each give him some gold and he would make them an idol, which he did (Exodus 32:5). When Moses came down from Mount Sinai and saw the golden calf, Aaron blamed the people of Israel, saying, "You know how prone these people are to evil. They said to me, 'Make us a god who will go before us'" (Exodus 32:22–23). Aaron's lie soon got bigger: "They gave me the gold, and I threw it into the fire, and out came this calf!" (v. 24).

I once told a friend that I could ski well. When we got to the slopes, I couldn't remember how to turn left. Why do we lie? Because we don't want others to know we're imperfect. We sin to avoid acknowledging our imperfections.

Another indication of perfectionism is legalism. Jesus confronted the legalism of the Pharisees, who believed that God wanted their perfection and that they could earn God's favor by being one hundred percent successful with a long list of dos and don'ts. He said to His listeners in the Sermon on the Mount: "Be perfect, therefore, as your heavenly Father is perfect" (Matthew 5:48), meaning: concentrate on the larger principles of loving God and others instead of concentrating on lists of dos and don'ts.

My friend Nancy had two renters living in her basement apartments. Alice always had a smile on her face, and she followed the rental agreement to the letter. She paid on time. She didn't have pets. She was "perfect." Jim, on the other hand, was always late paying his rent, and his girlfriend gave him a milk snake, which he kept in his room—without telling Nancy. One day, Alice—with a smile pasted on her face—told Nancy that Jim's snake got loose and had crawled into Alice's room. When she opened her door, the door squished the snake. Alice wanted Nancy to take care of the dead snake. Nancy hates snakes.

Which renter was better? Alice never said a kind word to anyone. She didn't care about anyone but herself. Jim loved Nancy's children. He was a great listener and conversationalist, and he cared about people.

The question about which is better is actually irrelevant. This life puzzle comes together when we realize that our perfection isn't the issue. We can never pay the rent. We need Jesus to pay it for us. His righteousness is our perfection. In the words of Martin Luther, *sola fide,* or faith alone, in Jesus' perfect sacrifice is what matters.

The Pharisees of Jesus' day were perfectionists. They thought they could follow God's law perfectly. But, as Jesus pointed out, they couldn't even follow all their own laws. He called them "hypocrites" (Matthew 23:13, 15, 23, 27, 29), "blind guides" (vv. 16, 24), and "snakes" (v. 33). On the outside they appeared righteous, but on the inside they were sinful (vv. 25, 28). Nicodemus was not just a Pharisee; he was also a teacher of the law (John 3:1–21) and a member of the Sanhedrin, the ruling council of the Jews. By all appearances, he was a successful and prominent person in his community. He visited Jesus at night to find out how to fit his notion of perfectionism with God's love.

But Jesus didn't tell him how to be more perfect or how to earn God's love or why he should give up on being loved by God. Jesus told Nicodemus that his perfection wasn't important. He told him that God loved him already. He told him that being born again is what matters. His message to each of us is the same.

CAN WE SOLVE THE PUZZLE WITH THE PIECES WE HAVE?

When we believe that God wants us to be perfect, we continually try harder to reach some elusive goal. We may even begin to resent God for imposing an expectation that we can't meet. Or we may give up totally because we believe we'll never achieve it. Either way, we're being a perfectionist. It's just that on one side we're still trying, and on the other side we've given up. Either way we are still measuring ourselves by a standard of 100 percent success.

Dieting brings out the worst of perfectionism in the best of us. We want to be perfect dieters. Unfortunately, human nature makes perfect dieting difficult. Some dieters keep trying hard and feeling disappointed that they fall short of perfection. Others reason like this: "I have to resist the temptation of eating a donut. If I fail and eat one donut, hey, I might as well eat the whole dozen."

Some students are all-or-nothing perfectionists. They want to get straight As. One type of perfectionist keeps trying despite failure and disappointment. Individuals of the other type reason, "If I get one B, hey, I might as well get all Fs because I've already failed."

People in close relationships sometimes become all-or-nothing perfectionists. Failing to meet the expectations of a parent, spouse, or boss causes some to keep trying harder. Others reason, "Since I can't meet their expectations, I'll prove their expectations are wrong by royally messing up." So whether we are successful or failing to be successful, we are measuring ourselves against a standard of 100 percent success.

I have worked with clients who can't stop trying. Through never-ending action they continually strive for perfection. I have also worked with folks whose desire for perfection has paralyzed them into a state of inaction. Their fear of failure, of making the wrong decision, of doing the wrong thing keeps them from doing anything, like sending out resumes.

SOLVING THE PUZZLE

To solve the puzzle we first need to think correctly about perfection. The correct blue sky puzzle piece is that God loves me just as I am. The correct green tree puzzle piece is that I rest in God's love for me and work out my salvation.

> Wonderful grace of Jesus,
> Reaching to all the lost,
> By it I have been pardoned,
> Saved to the uttermost;
> Chains have been torn asunder,
> Giving me liberty,

For the wonderful grace of Jesus reaches
me. (Haldor Lillenas)

We accept the wonderful grace of Jesus, we rest in God's love, and we work out our salvation. We take action. "The horse is made ready for the day of battle, but victory rests with the LORD" (Proverbs 21:31). As noted by the writer of Proverbs, letting God do His part is not enough; we also do our part. We have to prepare the horse. We get ready for the battle, and we trust God for the outcome. James said, "Faith by itself, if it is not accompanied by action, is dead" (James 2:17). Though God looks at Jesus' righteousness (1 Corinthians 1:30), He still expectantly waits for us to choose to live a life holy to Him. "But just as he who called you is holy, so be holy in all you do; for it is written: 'Be holy, because I am holy'" (1 Peter 1:15–16; see also Leviticus 11:44). A holy God demands a holy relationship with a set of holy behaviors.

HOLINESS VERSUS PERFECTIONISM

What do a spouse, a president, and a dog dish have in common? All are holy; each is "set apart" for an exclusive purpose. I am the spouse of only one person. The president is the head of only one nation. And only the dog uses the dog dish.

The sacred intimacy between spouses is exclusive. No one else is a part of that. So I wear a ring as a symbol of the holiness, or set-apartness, of marriage. It is no surprise that God uses marriage as a metaphor for our relationship with

Him. "As a bridegroom rejoices over his bride, so will your God rejoice over you" (Isaiah 62:5). As Christians, we have a "ring" on our finger. Holy living is nothing more than demonstrating to the world and all heavenly powers that we belong to God exclusively, that we've passed from the common to the sacred. Our daily behaviors show that we have been set apart to God.

I have a favorite dress that I "set apart" for special occasions. I wore it to my niece's wedding and to my nephew's graduation. My dress is a sign that something special is happening. Our lives are like my dress. Like the clothes we wear, our daily behaviors show God and the world around us that something special is happening: that we are trying to live our lives for God.

Paul used clothing as a metaphor for holy living: "Therefore, as God's chosen people, holy and dearly loved, clothe yourselves with compassion, kindness, humility, gentleness and patience" (Colossians 3:12).

Paul reminded Timothy that holy living is based entirely on God's grace (2 Timothy 1:8–9). Does holy living require perfection or sinlessness? No. A dog dish is not chosen for its perfection; it's chosen for its exclusivity. When God asks us to live a consecrated, holy life, He is asking us to continue to work toward growing more and more into Christlikeness (Ephesians 4:14).

The Bible has many examples of people who struggle repeatedly against their sinful nature: Abraham (Genesis 12:13; 20:2, 13), Samson (Judges 14:17; 16:7, 11, 13, 16–17), the people of Israel (Exodus 15:24; 16:2; 17:2). The point of the Old Testament is God's constancy, not the sinless lives of His people. The goal is holiness—to live a life wholly committed to God.

Jesus said that the greatest commandment is to love God wholly and to love your neighbor as yourself (Matthew 22:37–39). Paul picked up the same point when he wrote, "The only thing that counts is faith expressing itself through love" (Galatians 5:6). Thankfully, we're not on our own; we're in a partnership with God: "Continue to work out your salvation with fear and trembling, for it is God who works in you to will and to act according to his good purpose" (Philippians 2:12–13). The goal of our lives is to continue to strive to develop habits of holiness and to accept ourselves as we continue to learn and continue to commit ourselves more and more to God. We are on the road with God, and He loves us along the journey, not just when we reach the destination.

Some of us may have lost our hope for living this holy life due to our sin. But God continues to offer hope by promising to forgive us and also to purify us when we confess our sins (1 John 1:9). When we repent and turn from our sin, it will no longer be our downfall (Ezekiel 18:30).

God can use our mistakes for a larger good. Although Joseph's brothers sinned when they sold Joseph into slavery, many years later Joseph made this stunning acknowledgment: "You intended to harm me, but God intended it for good to accomplish what is now being done, the saving of many lives" (Genesis 50:20). We do not sin to give God an opportunity to do good, but God can do good despite our sin.

PLANNING FOR IMPERFECTION

In the field of counseling, "relapse prevention" refers to a plan for what to do *when*, not *if*, we fall back into old habits.

People who try to stop abusive drinking need a plan for what they will do when they fall back into drinking so they can get back on track as soon as possible. People who try to create new habits of thinking need to plan for what they will do when they fall back into old thinking patterns so they can stop the relapse and get back on track.

If a person expects perfection instead of holiness, the guilt of failure might propel the person into giving up. Relapse prevention is essential because, as Shakespeare noted, "to err is human." Relapse into old habits is expected. We know that "old habits die hard." We need to plan for our humanness, our "error."

I love to read novels. If I could get away with it that's all I'd do all day. But I know that I also need to read the Bible and spend time with God in prayer. It's not that I can't do both, but sometimes I want to read novels when I should be spending time with God. So I fight with myself about it, and sometimes novels win.

When I read a novel instead of the Bible, I could give up on reading the Bible. Or I could get myself back on track with a "relapse prevention" plan. My plan is to let each day be a new beginning. I start each day with a clean slate, with no shame for yesterday's relapse. I bring my guilt for sin and my human failures to God.

LOOKING AHEAD INSTEAD OF BEHIND

In daily living, this means that we accept where we are yet strive to move forward. As Paul wrote:

> Not that I have already obtained all this, or have already been made perfect, but I press on to take hold of that for which Christ Jesus took hold of me. Brothers, I do not consider myself yet to have taken hold of it. But one thing I do: Forgetting what is behind and straining toward what is ahead, I press on toward the goal to win the prize for which God has called me heavenward in Christ Jesus. (Philippians 3:12–14)

Psychologist Carl Rogers said, "When I accept myself just as I am, then I can change."

God loves us just as we are, and because we love Him we work on getting better at holy living (Ephesians 2:9–10; James 1:25; 1 John 3:9–10, 18).

Paul encouraged believers to "excel in gifts that build up the church" (1 Corinthians 14:12). In other words, take what God has given us and work at making it even better. The writer of Hebrews exhorts us to "show this same diligence to the very end, in order to make [our] hope sure" (Hebrews 6:11).

We accept ourselves as we are but keep working to get better.

GOD'S LOVE IS STABLE IN THE MIDST OF CHANGE

As a child playing capture the flag, I was afraid of being caught before I got to home base. Living in God's love is like always being on home base. We do not have to fear. If I base my self-esteem on my own performance, I have much to fear. But when God's love is my "home base," I need not fear anything. God's love remains constant even in the midst of changing circumstances.

Many people in the Bible had to stand firm in God's love for them. Shadrach, Meshach, and Abednego were thrown into a fiery furnace for refusing to worship Nebuchadnezzar's image (Daniel 3). They didn't know whether or not God would rescue them. They said to King Nebuchadnezzar,

> "If we are thrown into the blazing furnace,
> the God we serve is able to save us from
> it, and he will rescue us from your hand,
> O king. But even if he does not, we want
> you to know, O king, that we will not serve
> your gods or worship the image of gold
> you have set up." (Daniel 3:17–18)

Despite their uncertainty concerning the outcome, they were firmly committed to God. Like Shadrach, Meshach, and Abednego, we need to establish our confidence in God.

To plant a tree you dig a hole in the ground, place the tree in the hole, and surround the roots with good soil and fertilizer. However bad the soil is around the hole, the good soil and fertilizer is what the tree will feed on. In a way, God's love is like that—it's the source of our sustenance and our buffer.

ONE MORE WORRY ABOUT GOD'S LOVE

Sinful nature and human limitations aside, some Christians fear that God can't love them due to the immensity of the universe. People have been concerned about insignificance for ages. David cried out: "O LORD, what is man that you care for him, the son of man that you think of him?" (Psalm 144:3).

The Bible is clear that individuals matter. The gospel of John says that God loves everyone (John 3:16). Peter wrote that God wants everyone to come to repentance (2 Peter 3:9). Paul suggests that heavenly beings are watching the church as a kind of demonstration project (Ephesians 3:10). Imagine! Each of us is proving to Satan and his cohorts that God's way is better. The psalmist shows us a God who cares about each of our desires (Psalm 20:4). The parable of the lost sheep illustrates God's love for even just one (Luke 15:4–7). The parable of the prodigal son illustrates God's expectant waiting for each of us to come to Him (Luke 15:11–32).

I grew up in a family of four kids. I always wondered if my parents loved the others more than they loved me. I wasn't sure that I had anything special to offer my parents. Now that I've been a parent, I realize that it's possible to love each of my children wildly and without regard for what they offer me. Our sons are very different from each other, and I love each of them deeply. God loves us that way. He loves the peasant in the Pakistan Punjab as much as the queen of England. He loves the diamond miner in South Africa as much as He loves the Peruvian market woman in Machu Picchu. He loves me as much as He loves you.

God loves us in spite of our imperfections so that in His love we can be made more and more into the image of Christ.

QUESTIONS FOR GROUP DISCUSSION OR PERSONAL REFLECTION

■ Give an example of perfectionist thinking. Give an example of legalistic thinking.

■ How can you continue to work out your salvation with fear and trembling?

■ What habits have you already given up on changing? What relapse prevention plan can you put in place so that you can get back on track?

■ How would your life look different if you were confident of God's love at your core?

■ Has anyone ever believed in you when others did not? Compare that belief to God's steadfast love for you.

GOD'S CHARACTER
Predictable or Unpredictable?

BLUE SKY

So Satan went out from the presence of the LORD and afflicted Job with painful sores from the soles of his feet to the top of his head.... His wife said to him, "Are you still holding onto your integrity? Curse God and die." (Job 2:7–9)

Fear the LORD, you his holy people, for those who fear him lack nothing. The lions may grow weak and hungry, but those who seek the LORD lack no good thing. (Psalm 34:9–10)

GREEN TREE

He [Job] replied, "You are talking like a foolish woman. Shall we accept good from God, and not trouble?" (Job 2:10)

I saw under the altar the souls of those who had been slain because of the word of God and the testimony they had maintained. (Revelation 6:9)

COUNSELOR & CLIENT CONVERSATION

ME: You're not sure you can trust God to play by your rules.

CAROL: Well, I thought they were His rules too.

ME: But they aren't?

CAROL: They don't seem to be.

ME: So when bad things happen you feel that God isn't playing by the rules.

CAROL: Right. I keep wondering when the other shoe will drop.

ME: It's hard to trust a God who might drop a shoe at any moment!

CAROL: Yes, trust doesn't describe our relationship!

ME: Trust is built on predictability. Is God unpredictable?

CAROL: In the worst way!

ME: What would it take to trust God more?

CAROL: If He were more predictable, that would help.

ME: So if God followed more of the rules, He'd be more predictable and you could trust Him more?

CAROL: Yes. I can only trust a God who is predictable. I can't trust one who isn't.

OUR FAMILY LIKES TO CLIMB "FOURTEENERS." Fourteeners are Colorado mountains that are 14,000 feet tall or more. One year we were climbing Mount Lindsey in the San Juan mountains, which is bear country. We were very careful to keep all food out of our tents, to hang our garbage in a tree far from our camp, and to hang tomorrow's lunch high up in a tree. No sooner had we zipped up our tents to go to sleep than a big bear came snuffling around our tent. We made some noise and he left. Five minutes later, we heard a big tree branch crack. The next morning a big brown bear was sleeping next to our lunch bag ripped open and almost empty. We had done everything we were supposed to do. Sometimes the unexpected happens despite our best efforts.

MOST OF THE TIME, THE EXPECTED HAPPENS

But most of our efforts pay off and life just cooks along as expected. This predictability helps us negotiate life. We expect the chair to hold us when we sit on it. We expect objects to fall toward earth. We expect the sun to rise and set every day (or, as my scientist husband corrects, we expect the earth to turn). We expect spring to follow winter. We expect bears to leave our lunch alone. When some of these expectations are violated, we don't get unduly upset.

When our youngest son was ten or so, he wanted to show us a great skiing move. "Watch me!" he yelled as he proceeded to "clothesline" himself on an unexpected rope across his path. He wasn't scarred by the unusual event. He isn't an overly cautious skier today. He still enjoys variety and adventure despite his early experience.

THE UNEXPECTED MAKES US DOUBT IF WE CAN TRUST GOD

However, we don't want major surprises when it comes to certain expectations. We expect to have a job. We expect to be able to retire. We expect our children to outlive us. When we lose a job, we might question what God is up to. When we lose a chunk of our savings to a swindler, we might wonder why God didn't come to our rescue. When a child dies, we might be mad at God because we know He could have prevented the death. For those who believe that God is in control, big surprises cause us to wonder if we can trust God. We believe that the world should be fair, that justice or mercy must triumph (especially for us).

Many Christians have turned from God when something bad happened. Divorce. Death. An economic setback. A baby born with a challenging life ahead. When such things happen, some Christians feel as if God has let them down, as if He has betrayed an agreement they had with Him. People state the agreement differently, but it goes something like this: "If I live my life for God, God needs to bless me."

GIDEON DIDN'T TRUST GOD

Gideon believed the people of Israel had such an agreement with God. But because he lived when the Midianites were oppressing Israel, he didn't believe that God was holding up His side of the bargain. When an angel came to Gideon saying, "The LORD is with you," Gideon responded:

> "But sir," Gideon replied, "if the LORD is
> with us, why has all this happened to us?
> Where are all his wonders that our fathers
> told us about when they said, 'Did not the
> LORD bring us up out of Egypt?' But now
> the LORD has abandoned us and put us into
> the hand of Midian." (Judges 6:13)

I can hear Gideon's contempt for what the angel said. It sure didn't look to him as if God was with Israel. Gideon believed that if God was with Israel, the Midianites wouldn't be oppressing them.

Suffering makes us wonder if God is holding up His side of the bargain. We aren't the only ones to wonder. Peter wrote to Christians who believed that suffering meant something was wrong. Peter told them (and us) to not "be surprised at the painful trial you are suffering, as though something strange were happening to you" (1 Peter 4:12). Suffering doesn't mean that something's wrong. But it feels that way.

I have trouble opening childproof caps. One day I was struggling to open some decongestant and the bottle tipped over. Despite my best efforts to pick up all the pills quickly, our three-pound Chihuahua swallowed one. For the rest of the day, he hallucinated and barked at the white wall. My reaction was, "Poor guy, he shouldn't have to go through that." But why not?

It doesn't take long for a newborn baby to experience the suffering of our world through hunger, sickness, cold, and heat. As much as we try to shield our children (or dogs) from the evil of the world, their peers (or sometimes their family) manage to expose them to teasing, cheating, lying, criticism, goading, and even physical harm. There is no doubt that suffering exists in our world.

And sometimes we might blame God.

PROVERBS: THE RULEBOOK FOR LIFE

Where do we develop the expectation that suffering is unexpected and that only good things should come to those the Lord loves? One place is the book of Proverbs, which is considered to be God's "rulebook" or "playbook" for life. In it, we find out how to live wisely so that we will be blessed, and we start to think of its instructions in terms of cause and effect. Cause: Follow God. Effect: Get blessed. Cause: Work hard. Effect: Get rich. We find this cause and effect relationship over and over in Proverbs:

"Lazy hands make a man poor, but diligent hands bring wealth" (10:4).

"He who works his land will have abundant food, but he who chases fantasies lacks judgment" (12:11).

"Diligent hands will rule, but laziness ends in slave labor" (12:24).

"The sluggard craves and gets nothing, but the desires of the diligent are fully satisfied" (13:4).

"All hard work brings a profit, but mere talk leads only to poverty" (14:23).

It is understandable why we believe we have a contract with God in which we do this and God does that.

ANOTHER RULE FOR LIVING

Another "contract" we believe that we have with God is that having many advisors guarantees good decisions. "For lack of guidance a nation falls, but many advisers make victory sure" (Proverbs 11:14). Cause: Many advisors. Effect: Good decisions that result in victory.

However, the number of advisors doesn't always relate to the wisdom of a decision and victory. This cause and effect relationship doesn't always bear out. For example, in ancient Israel four hundred prophets predicted a successful campaign against the Arameans, and one prophet of God predicted disaster (1 Kings 22). Ahab decided to follow the four hundred prophets and died in battle. Why did the great number of Ahab's advisors not result in victory as Proverbs 11:14 suggests? Do Ahab's advisors disprove Proverbs 11:14?

No. Proverbs 11:14 describes only one aspect of decision-making and advisors. Other aspects determine the outcome of a decision. First, the number of advisors makes a difference only if some of them are wise: "The plans of the righteous are just, but the advice of the wicked is deceitful" (12:5). So if we have many *wise* advisors are we home free? Proverbs goes on to say that we have to seek advice and listen to it (12:15; 19:20; 20:18.) Furthermore, God trumps all advisors: "There is no wisdom, no insight, no plan that can succeed against the LORD" (21:30). The "rule" that "many advisers make victory sure" (11:14) is affected by other factors.

When we took our sons skiing for the first time, our oldest was concerned about all the people whizzing past him. I told him not to worry because the uphill skier is responsible to watch for anyone downhill. Five minutes later, a woman plowed into him. Obviously, other factors were at work besides "the rule."

JOB: WHEN CAUSE AND EFFECT ARE UNRELATED

The book of Job captures one man's struggle when he discovered that causes don't always have predictable effects and that our rules aren't always God's rules.

When Satan entered the presence of God, God encouraged him to notice His servant Job. Satan baited God, insisting that Job lived a holy life only because God had put a hedge around him. "You have blessed the work of his hands . . . But stretch out your hand and strike everything he has, and he will surely curse you to your face" (Job 1:10–11). After receiving permission from God to strike Job's family and his possessions, he went out from God's presence and caused horrendous tragedies against Job. But Job refused to curse God. Incredibly, he worshiped God instead!

> Then [Job] fell to the ground in worship
> and said: "Naked I came from my mother's
> womb, and naked I will depart. The LORD
> gave and the LORD has taken away; may

> the name of the LORD be praised." In all
> this, Job did not sin by charging God with
> wrongdoing. (Job 1:20–21)

So Satan returned to God's presence and again God encouraged Satan to notice His servant Job and his blameless response to tragedy. Satan said, "A man will give all he has for his own life. But stretch out your hand and strike his flesh and bones and he will surely curse you to your face" (Job 2:4).

God allowed Satan to afflict Job with sores but did not let Satan take Job's life. So Job was covered in painful sores from head to toe. Job and his wife responded differently. Each response illustrates a different puzzle piece.

> Then Job took a piece of broken pottery
> and scraped himself with it as he sat
> among the ashes. His wife said to him,
> "Are you still holding on to your integrity?
> Curse God and die!" He replied, "You are
> talking like a foolish woman. Shall we
> accept good from God, and not trouble?"
> In all this, Job did not sin in what he said.
> (Job 2:8–10)

THE PUZZLE PIECES

Job's wife chose the blue sky piece of the puzzle.

She held onto the idea of cause and effect. God must act predictably. If we follow Him wholeheartedly, He must bless us. She tells Job to curse God and die (Job 2:9) because she believed that God had broken His promise. Her belief system of predictability went something like this: God guaranteed that if I follow His wisdom He will bless me. In order for me to trust Him, God must limit Himself to predictable behaviors.

Job chose the green tree piece of the puzzle. God can do anything He wants and is not limited by human expectations. Despite his pain, Job understood that we cannot limit God's behaviors. Job realized there are no guarantees. He understood that God is free to act however He chooses.

Our Christian task is to fit these two puzzle pieces together.

Some Christians don't want both pieces. They would rather throw out Job's piece of the puzzle. They want God to be predictable because they fear that God's unpredictability means there are no guarantees; there is only chaos. When they experience unexpected trouble, as Job's wife did, they curse God for not honoring the "guarantee." But when God acts outside the bounds of the rulebook in Proverbs, does that mean the rulebook is invalid? Not at all.

One day my husband and I were visiting the Jerusalem zoo when suddenly people started yelling in Hebrew. We had no clue what they were saying, but someone finally translated for us. A zoo worker had neglected to close the cage and the tiger had gotten loose. Thankfully, the tiger was caught and locked up again.

The tiger getting loose (the exception) doesn't mean that the tiger will typically be loose (the rule.) The tiger getting loose is in fact a proof of the unusualness of typical zoo protocol. Hence, the exception "proves" that the rule exists. Because exceptions happen rarely and the rule occurs more frequently, the rule is established as a rule.

Some Christians grab the opposite puzzle piece and struggle. They prefer predictability. And generally life is predictable. The balancing message of Job is that God does what He chooses.

So what do we do when we encounter surprises? What do we do when we don't get the expected outcomes? What do we do when we didn't get a blessing from God for our good behavior? Do we stop trusting God? Do we give up trying? No, we trust God to show His love in surprising ways. We expect the cause/effect relationships as well as surprises, and we continue to trust God.

ASLAN, A WILD LION

The Lion, the Witch, and the Wardrobe by C. S. Lewis is an allegory in which Aslan, a lion, represents Jesus. Through Aslan, Lewis makes clear an important truth about God—He is not tame.

Like Aslan, God is not tamed by our requests. Our rules don't whip Him into shape. He does not do our bidding. As Lord of this universe, we do His. His rule prevails. Thankfully, He's a loving God. Like Aslan, Jesus died to pay our debts.

WHY DOESN'T GOD FOLLOW THE RULES HE SET IN MOTION?

If God infused His cause-and-effect wisdom into the world, why does He act unpredictably? One reason is that God's goal is larger than our happiness. We are part of God's strategy to take back the earth from Satan, "the prince of this world" (John 12:31). When we watch the evening news, we know that the world is Satan's realm. But God is working to change the ruling regime. God is infiltrating Satan's realm on earth to win the ultimate battle for souls.

THE SPIRITUAL BATTLE GOING ON FOR OUR SOULS

This is a spiritual battle, not physical. As Paul wrote: "For our struggle is not against flesh and blood, but against the rulers, against the authorities, against the powers of this dark world and against the spiritual forces of evil in the heavenly realms" (Ephesians 6:12). Paul's intent "was that now, through the church, the manifold wisdom of God should be made known to the rulers and authorities in the heavenly realms, according to his eternal purpose, which he accomplished in Christ Jesus our Lord" (Ephesians 3:10–11). The church is a live demonstration, and spiritual beings are watching what the church does. Consider what we are demonstrating: that love works better than hate, that good works better than evil, that free will works better than control. When it seems as if life is nothing more than chaos, the reality is that we are part of a struggle between God and Satan. The battle is not being fought by nations for world dominance; it's being waged by believers who willingly submit to God's supremacy over their hearts, souls, minds, and bodies.

Jesus referred to this spiritual battle when He taught about the kingdom of God. "Kingdom" is usually a political and geographical term. But Jesus made clear that His kingdom is not tied to geographical boundaries. He said, "My kingdom is not of this world . . . But now my kingdom is from another place" (John 18:36). And "The kingdom of God is within you" (Luke 17:21). Jesus told Nicodemus, "I tell you the truth, no one can see the kingdom of God unless he is born again" (John 3:3). This is a spiritual kingdom.

We see examples of this cosmic struggle in Christian art forms. In *The Lion, the Witch, and the Wardrobe*, Aslan infiltrated Narnia. In Mel Gibson's movie "The Passion of the Christ," we get the full sense that God has a grand plan in which Jesus plays the central role. At the beginning, Jesus crushed a serpent's head. As the film progresses, we sense that God and Satan are engaged in a cosmic struggle. Satan thinks that Jesus' death is in his favor. It turns out that it's in God's favor. By the end, Satan is the one in agony.

The Bible includes many references to Satan fighting for our souls, our behaviors, our choices. The prophet Zechariah gave this description:

> Then he showed me Joshua the high priest standing before the angel of the LORD, and Satan standing at his right side to accuse him. The LORD said to Satan, "The LORD rebuke you, Satan! The LORD, who has

chosen Jerusalem, rebuke you! Is not this
man a burning stick snatched from the
fire?" (3:1–2)

Jesus gave this description of Satan's attempt to destroy
Peter's faith: "Simon, Simon, Satan has asked to sift you as
wheat. But I have prayed for you, Simon, that your faith may
not fail. And when you have turned back, strengthen your
brothers" (Luke 22:31). The book of Revelation describes
the final battle between God and Satan:

I saw heaven standing open and there
before me was a white horse, whose rider
is called Faithful and True. With justice
he judges and makes war. . . . Then I saw
the beast and the kings of the earth and
their armies gathered together to make
war against the rider on the horse and his
army. (19:11, 19)

God and Satan are in a contest to win souls for eternity.
The Book of Revelation assures us that God is going to
conquer all. At the end of history, no one will wonder if
Satan's way is better than God's. Everyone will know that
God's way is best. In the meantime, we're to demonstrate
that God's way is best by squarely aligning ourselves on
God's side through holy living.

In *The Grinch Who Stole Christmas*, Dr. Seuss introduced
readers to the Whos, who are inhabitants of a snowflake in
another world. Like the Whos, we too are part of a larger

world. Our lives get played out in the material world, but the spiritual world is the larger reality.

But none of us volunteered for this offensive. Why do we have to suffer? Why does God allow bad things to happen that aren't "our fault"? How is it fair that we get caught in the crossfire of this cosmic battle?

One reason for suffering is that we live in Satan's realm, and he causes pain. We saw that in Job's life (Job 1–2).

PAIN CAUSED BY SOMEONE ELSE'S BAD CHOICES

Sometimes we reap the consequences of someone else's bad choices. Since Adam and Eve sinned, sin reigns in the world and we all suffer for it. Even the earth suffers. As Paul wrote, "The whole creation has been groaning as in the pains of childbirth right up to the present time" (Romans 8:22).

Pain can occur because one of our ancestors sinned, and the effects have rippled through the generations. A father who drinks away all his money will certainly affect his children and his children's children. A grandmother who abuses her children will create a cycle of abuse that will continue through the generations until one person decides to break the cycle. Even though these issues may not be our fault, they are our responsibility. We do have to deal with them.

PAIN CAUSED BY OUR OWN BAD CHOICES

Another reason for pain is that we are reaping the

consequences of our own bad choices. God is the master of "tough love." David slept with Bathsheba when she was married to another man, and she became pregnant. The prophet Nathan told David, "Because by doing this you have made the enemies of the LORD show utter contempt, the son born to you will die" (2 Samuel 12:14). God loved David and Bathsheba, but He let them suffer the consequences of their actions. He does the same with us. In the New Testament, we read, "Our fathers disciplined us for a little while as they thought best; but God disciplines us for our good, that we may share in his holiness. No discipline seems pleasant at the time, but painful. Later on, however, it produces a harvest of righteousness and peace for those who have been trained by it" (Hebrews 12:10–11).

PAIN CAN HELP US GROW

God also uses pain to form us into Christ's likeness. Paul said, "We also rejoice in our sufferings, because we know that suffering produces perseverance; perseverance, character; and character, hope. And hope does not disappoint us, because God has poured out his love into our hearts by the Holy Spirit, whom he has given us" (Romans 5:3–5). He is not talking about getting a hangnail or being late for work. He is talking about unmet expectations. He's talking about being hated for being a Christian when we expected to be respected. He's talking about losing a job when we expected to have one. He's talking about the death of a loved one before it was "supposed" to happen. The ultimate goal is our maturity: "Consider it pure joy, my brothers, whenever you face trials of many kinds, because you know that the testing of your faith develops perseverance. Perseverance must finish its work so that you may be mature and complete, not lacking anything" (James 1:2–3).

PAIN INCREASES OUR ABILITY TO SYMPATHIZE WITH OTHERS

Another reason for pain is that it helps us sympathize with and serve others: "Praise be to the God and Father of our Lord Jesus Christ, the Father of compassion and the God of all comfort, who comforts us in all our troubles, so that we can comfort those in any trouble with the comfort we ourselves have received from God" (2 Corinthians 1:3–4).

GOD REMAINS IN CONTROL

It is clear from Job's life that God allowed bad things to happen to him. But God is clear that He controls what Satan can and can't do. Nothing happens without His permission.

In the book of 1 Kings, a prophet of God named Micaiah gave us yet another example of God exercising control over Satan's demons:

> "Therefore hear the word of the LORD: I saw the LORD sitting on his throne with all the host of heaven standing around him on his right and on his left. And the LORD said, 'Who will entice Ahab into attacking

Ramoth Gilead and going to his death there?'

"One suggested this, and another that. Finally, a spirit came forward, stood before the LORD and said, 'I will entice him.'

"'By what means?' the LORD asked.

"'I will go out and be a lying spirit in the mouths of all his prophets,' he said.

"'You will succeed in enticing him,' said the LORD. 'Go and do it.'

"So now the LORD has put a lying spirit in the mouths of all these prophets of yours. The LORD has decreed disaster for you." (22:19–23)

God alone allows lying spirits to go out and fool people. It's kind of surprising that God doesn't try to cover up His part in Job's suffering or in allowing lying spirits to fool Ahab. He isn't at all ashamed of these facts. Humans are more embarrassed by the so-called problem of pain than God is.

GOD IS LOVE

God unashamedly claims sovereign control of the universe. He also makes an unashamed claim to love us despite all the pain resulting from the evil of the world. The Bible says, "God is love" (1 John 4:8). Love is the essence of who God is. Despite the tragedy that befalls us, despite the pain that we endure, despite the excruciating agonies suffered by humanity perpetrated by other humans, God is in control and He loves us. God's love is so certain that we can take it to the bank: "And so we know and rely on the love God has for us. God is love. Whoever lives in love lives in God, and God in him" (1 John 4:16). The blue sky piece of the puzzle is the pain in the world. The green tree piece is God's love for us. People have tried for ages to make these pieces mutually exclusive. They cannot reconcile a loving, all-powerful God with a pain-filled world. People argue that God can't be both all-loving *and* all-powerful. They assume that God would never allow all the pain in the world if He could prevent it. Yet in the Bible, we see both puzzle pieces side by side and fitting together. For God, love and pain are not mutually exclusive. Both puzzle pieces fit together.

FAITH IS BELIEVING IN GOD'S LOVE
WHEN THE EVIDENCE POINTS IN THE OPPOSITE DIRECTION

Some of the most poignant expressions of faith come in the midst of pain. Habakkuk argued with God about the coming Babylonian invasion because of the Babylonians' ruthlessness. Throughout most of the book, he complains about the unfairness of using very evil people to punish the "not so evil" Israelites. Habakkuk complained to God: "Why are you silent while the wicked swallow up those more righteous than themselves?" (Habakkuk 1:13). God answered that "the righteous will live by his faith" (2:4). Habakkuk's response is one of the most piercing statements of faith in the Bible:

> Though the fig tree does not bud and there
> are no grapes on the vines, though the olive
> crop fails and the fields produce no food,
> though there are no sheep in the pen and
> no cattle in the stalls, yet I will rejoice in the
> LORD, I will be joyful in God my Savior. The
> Sovereign LORD is my strength; he makes
> my feet like the feet of a deer, he enables me
> to go on the heights. (3:17–19)

Jeremiah also faced invasion. When the Babylonians invaded and most of the Israelites were exiled to Babylon, Jeremiah poured out his intense sorrow in the book of Lamentations. Mixed with his sorrow and great pain are professions of great faith:

> I remember my affliction and my wandering,
> the bitterness and the gall. I well remember
> them, and my soul is downcast within me.
> Yet this I call to mind and therefore I have
> hope: Because of the LORD's great love we
> are not consumed, for his compassions
> never fail. They are new every morning;
> great is your faithfulness. I say to myself,
> "The LORD is my portion; therefore I will
> wait for him." The LORD is good to those
> whose hope is in him, to the one who
> seeks him; it is good to wait quietly for
> the salvation of the LORD. (Lamentations
> 3:19–26)

In the 1970s, my husband and I and some friends traveled by bus across Afghanistan. Between Kabul and Kandahar, most of the road is built high so that the snow will blow off in the winter. During the night, our driver fell asleep and we flew off the road. Thankfully, it happened at one of the rare spots where the road wasn't built up. But the bus axle broke, so in the middle of the night all the passengers piled out while the driver patched the axle together so the bus could limp to Kandahar. The best part of the experience (besides being alive!) happened at dawn when a tribe of nomads came across the desert, circled their camels, and in fifteen minutes had their tents up and their cooking fires going to warm their breakfast chai. The tribe engaged in its daily activities as if nothing were wrong, as if we hadn't just escaped death by a hair, as if a bus weren't disabled in their back yard. The normalcy of it all was comforting. Faith in God brought to Habakkuk and Jeremiah, and also brings to us, that same sense of normalcy in the midst of chaos.

"GOD WORKS FOR THE GOOD OF THOSE WHO LOVE HIM" ROMANS 8:28

We have faith in God that He loves us in the midst of our pain. We also have faith in God to give our pain some meaning, to use it for something. God, in His amazing, all-encompassing knowledge, is able to make all the pains in the world work for good. My husband liked to play chess with our kids when they were little, and he became an expert at turning all their moves to their advantage so they could win. To pull that off, he had to see the big picture—to know where the game was going and be able to think many moves ahead. God does that. He works for our good in the midst of pain. He's been doing it for a long time.

Job recognized that pain can be part of God's loving plan. Job's wife didn't allow God the right to act outside of her imposed limits. We need to accept each puzzle piece and live in the tension between them. Job's wife's expectations for health, family, and wealth were shattered. She believed that if God did not deliver these things, He wasn't to be trusted. Job looked at it differently. He saw that God was at liberty to do as He pleases within the confines of His love.

HOW DO I LIVE WITH GOD'S RIGHT TO DO WHAT HE WANTS?

If we accept that God can do what He wants, we have to be ready for the worst. We also have to be ready for the best. But how do we stay "ready" for such opposites? One way is to constantly expect the worst so it doesn't blindside us. One way is to focus on what is best in the world so we can stay in our "happy place." Which should we do?

I worked with a client who got caught in the middle of a hold up. She came to me because she was anxious all the time. She worried about when something bad would happen to her next. She was constantly vigilant. She was trying to make sure nothing bad would ever happen to her again. She was overcome by her constant fear.

I worked with another client who had suffered horrible things but could only admit to the good in the world. Everything was always wonderful. Everything was always working out. She spent most of her time reading novels and watching movies. She couldn't spend too much time in the "real world" of people and work because it reminded her of the bad in the world. She was stuck in her fantasy that the world had to be all good.

I have on my desk a picture that another client gave me—that of a spectacular rainbow with a stormy sky in the background. The caption reads: "It takes both rain and sunshine to make a rainbow." The picture captures truth. There is both good and evil in the world. And we focus on both.

We focus on both because both happen. Wonderful good happens every day: blazing sunsets, towering mountains, and dramatic storms, the miracle of life, a child's first steps (whether it's the first steps in life or the steps down an aisle), the comforting touch of a friend when we need it. And side by side, beauty coexists with murder, hurricanes, terrorism, war, injustice, illness, and divorce.

Focusing on the worst alone results in fear, anxiety, and depression. Focusing on the good alone results in fantasy. Both can result in inaction. What's the point of trying to change homelessness if we're stuck with it? Why work on solving the problem of homelessness if homelessness doesn't exist?

HOW DO WE FOCUS ON BOTH?

I have heard a story about a big storm that littered a beach with thousands of starfish. A little boy was throwing starfish back when a cynical man asked, "There are millions of starfish on this beach. You'll never be able to help them all. What difference does it make?" The boy responded while he threw a starfish in the ocean: "It makes a difference for that one."

We focus on both the good and the bad by doing what we can to fix the bad. Our pastor, Chuck Orwiler, says, "God doesn't give us the job of fixing a broken world. That's His job."

HOPE IS THE GLUE THAT KEEPS THE PUZZLE PIECES TOGETHER

One of the main messages of the *Fellowship of the Ring* by J. R. R. Tolkien is *Dum vita est spes est,* "While there is life there is hope." Hope is a biblical principle that we don't hear much about but which is vitally important to reconciling the good and the bad. Job said, "Though he slay me yet will I hope" (Job 13:15). Jeremiah understood that hope depends on God's positive plans for our future: "'For I know the plans I have for you,' declares the LORD, 'plans to prosper you and not to harm you, plans to give you hope and a future'" (Jeremiah 29:11). Hope is vitally important to making it through tough times. That's why hope is listed in the "hall of fame" of Christian virtues: "We know that suffering produces perseverance; perseverance, character; and character, hope. And hope does not disappoint us" (Romans 5:3–5), and "These three remain: faith, hope, and love" (1 Corinthians 13:13).

Hope helps us negotiate the puzzle of an evil and good world. Paul commended the Thessalonians for their "endurance inspired by hope in our Lord Jesus Christ"

(1 Thessalonians 1:3). Hope is an anchor: "We have this hope as an anchor for the soul, firm and secure" (Hebrews 6:19). Faith is taking hope one step further: "Faith is being sure of what we hope for" (Hebrews 11:1). The book of Revelation speaks to our ultimate hope: "He will wipe every tear from their eyes. There will be no more death or mourning or crying or pain, for the old order of things has passed away" (21:4).

During World War II, homeless children were unable to sleep until someone began letting them sleep with bread. Bread reminded them of their hope, "Today I ate and I will eat again tomorrow."[15] Hope helps us negotiate pain.

EVIL + GOOD = A NEW PERSPECTIVE

We have a different perspective on the good when we juxtapose it with pain. When bad happens, we suddenly realize how good things are. As Joni Mitchell sang, "You don't know what you've got 'til it's gone." Sunsets are particularly beautiful to me after a hard day at work. A majestic mountain or endless waves on a beach feed my soul when I'm hurting.

So how do we survive in an out-of-control world of pain? Hang onto God's love, hang onto His control, take control and responsibility where we can, and enjoy the ride as much as possible. Living in this world is like riding a roller coaster. We ride to the heights and we ride out the lows and we hang on tight to God's love.

The writer of Ecclesiastes knew that life isn't fair when bad things happen to good people. He wrote,

There is something else meaningless that
occurs on earth: righteous men who get
what the wicked deserve, and wicked men
who get what the righteous deserve. This
too, I say, is meaningless. (8:14)

But he also recognized that the good and the bad both
come from God:

When times are good, be happy; but when
times are bad, consider: God has made the
one as well as the other. (7:14)

WHAT KIND OF PUZZLE IS THIS?

God created the world with an underlying sense of
predictability. Generally, God blesses our efforts. However,
He doesn't limit Himself to predictable behaviors. God is
free to act in whatever way furthers His purpose within
the confines of His loving character. Sometimes bad things
happen to good people. When we feel let down by God's
unpredictability, our task is to live in the tension of these
opposites.

QUESTIONS FOR GROUP DISCUSSION OR PERSONAL REFLECTION

- Have you ever felt that God let you down? That He didn't meet one of His guarantees to you? How?

- How have you dealt with your crushed expectations? In what other ways can you deal with your crushed expectations? What do you think God was up to when He acted unpredictably with you?

- In the war for souls, what is Satan's strategy? What is God's strategy? Are you aware of the contest for your soul? Why did Job's behaviors matter? Why do ours?

- How do you explain the pain in the world? Which do you focus on: the good or the pain in life? Why?

GOD'S WILL

Active Seeking or Passive Waiting?

BLUE SKY

The LORD Almighty has sworn, "Surely, as I have planned, so it will be, and as I have purposed, so it will stand. For the LORD Almighty has purposed, and who can thwart him? His hand is stretched out, and who can turn it back?" (Isaiah 14:24, 27)

GREEN TREE

Jesus told his disciples a parable to show them that they should always pray and not give up.... "'Because this widow keeps bothering me, I will see that she gets justice, so that she won't eventually wear me out with her coming!'" (Luke 18:1, 5)

COUNSELOR & CLIENT CONVERSATION

ME: One of the things you want God to help you with is making a decision about what to do with your life.

CAROL: Yes, and He seems so silent.

ME: What have you done to get an answer from Him?

CAROL: I've prayed.

ME: Anything else?

CAROL: No, I'm afraid of doing anything else because it might be the wrong thing.

ME: What if you looked in the paper and sent out a few resumes to places that look interesting to you?

CAROL: But what if those aren't the things that God wants me to do?

ME: And what if they are?

CAROL: I don't want to risk doing the wrong thing and making God mad.

ME: So the best way to not make God mad is to be more passive and wait for Him....because being active might make Him mad?

CAROL: Yes, God's happy when I'm passive and God's unhappy when I'm active. It's pretty simple that way.

IN A STORY I HEARD WHEN I WAS YOUNG, A FATHER offered dimes to each of his two sons. The aggressive son took the shiny one and left the duller one for his more passive brother. Later the boys learned that the duller coin was older and worth more than the shiny one. The moral I took from the story was, don't be pushy, accept what is given to you, appearances can be deceiving, what you want may not be the best.

In another story, a man ran an orphanage. One evening, he sat all the orphans down for supper even though the money and food were gone. They prayed and thanked God for the non-existent food. After the "Amen," they heard a knock on the door. A grocery truck had broken down nearby, and the driver wanted to know if the orphanage could use the food before it spoiled.

I've heard countless other stories of God's provision in response to the prayers of Christians. In many of the stories, all they did was pray and God answered. I came to believe that God was more likely to reward passivity than "pushiness" and began waiting for God to bring me what I needed.

DIRECTION

In college, I needed career direction. I prayed and waited. I searched the Bible for verses that would show me how God was going to lead me to a particular career. Was He going to call me audibly? Was He going to lead me through a particular Bible verse? Was He going to lead me through wise counsel from my parents?

I became increasingly frustrated because I found so little in the Bible about how this calling or leading was going to work. I worried that I was looking in the wrong places or listening in the wrong ways. Not until many years later did I figure out that the Bible has little to say about "calling" or "leading" in regard to career decisions.

Haddon Robinson has this to say:

> We must face the fact: "How do you know the will of God in making life's decisions?" is not a biblical question! The Bible never tells us to ask it. The Bible never gives us direction in answering it. And the pursuit of some personalized version of the "will of God" often leads us toward disobedience. When we find ourselves facing the tough choices in life—those day-in, day-out decisions that make up the very fabric of our existence—we shouldn't seek special messages from God. Instead, we should ask, "How do we develop the skills necessary to make wise and prudent choices?"
>
> The Bible does speak to that question— at length. We should not turn to Scripture in search of a detailed road map. The Bible is not so much a map as it is a compass. It doesn't give us specifics but it does provide direction.[16]

CALLING

Jeremiah was appointed to be a prophet (Jeremiah 1:5), and Paul was called to be an apostle (Romans 1:1). Other than these, the Bible has few references to anyone being called to a particular profession. Most instances of the word "call" involve being called into a relationship with God. We are *called* from darkness into light. "You are a chosen people, a royal priesthood, a holy nation, a people belonging to God, that you may declare the praises of him who called you out of darkness into his wonderful light" (1 Peter 2:9). We are *called* to justification. "And those he predestined, he also called; those he called, he also justified; those he justified, he also glorified" (Romans 8:30). We are *called* to live a life of holiness. "For God did not call us to be impure, but to live a holy life" (1 Thessalonians 4:7).

The same is true of the word "lead." It refers to living in relationship with God. "*Lead* me in a straight path" (Psalm 27:11). "*Lead* me in the way everlasting" (Psalm 139:24). "*Lead* us not into temptation" (Matthew 6:13). "So the law was put in charge to *lead* us to Christ" (Galatians 3:24).

One thing is certain: we are called to live a life holy to God. Living a holy life is one of the most important calls on your life.

> So many times you will see people wringing their hands, and saying, "I want to know what my Mission in life is," all the while they are cutting people off on the highway, refusing to give time to people, punishing

their mate for having hurt their feelings, and lying about what they did. And it will seem to you that the angels must laugh to see this spectacle. For these people, wringing their hands, their Mission was right there, on the freeway, in the interruption, in the hurt, and at the confrontation.[17]

However, most people want a more specific calling than holiness. We want to know specifically what career God wants us to pursue. We yearn for the specific call of God's prophets.

Jonah had a specific word from the LORD—preach to the Ninevites—but the Ninevites were violent people, and Israel was their enemy. Jonah knew God would be forgiving and compassionate to the Ninevites (Jonah 4:1–3) and he hated the Ninevites, so he ran in the opposite direction. He didn't want to make the Ninevites aware of their opportunity for repentance. It would be like going to the person who assaulted you and telling him or her about the good news of Jesus. Jonah wanted the Ninevites dead. Only after being rescued from death by a fish did Jonah finally decide to obey the word of the LORD. The Ninevites repented and God forgave them. (This, apparently, was God's plan all along, as Jonah suspected.)

The focal point of the book of Jonah was not Jonah's refusal to follow the proper career path; it was his smug self-righteousness. Jonah might have been willing to go elsewhere, just not to Ninevah. He thought God's mercies should extend only to "good" Israelites, not to "sinful"

Ninevites. Jonah's sin was his failure to live a holy life submitted to God. He forgot that he belonged to God and that belonging to God means loving and forgiving as God bids.

SOME CAREERS AREN'T OPTIONS

Even though Jonah's sin did not involve career choice, there are sinful careers. For example, being a hit man serves one man's selfish goals for power and control. Being a prostitute misdirects sexuality, which should be expressed in the context of marriage. However, most of us don't struggle with choosing a sinful or non-sinful career. We struggle with how to get some specific direction from God because we don't want to sin unintentionally.

Christians sometimes fear that their choices will make or break God's plan in history. Jonah's experience makes clear that God is able to move forward with or without us, or in spite of us. Even though Jonah initially refused to go to Nineveh, God moved His plan forward nonetheless. He may have been disappointed, but He was not checkmated by Jonah's choice.

THE PUZZLE: ACTIVITY OR PASSIVITY?

The blue sky piece of this life puzzle is that God will move history forward regardless of my choices. "The LORD works out everything for his own ends" (Proverbs 16:4).

The LORD Almighty has sworn, "Surely, as

I have planned, so it will be, and as I have purposed, so it will stand. For the LORD Almighty has purposed, and who can thwart him? His hand is stretched out, and who can turn it back?" (Isaiah 14:24, 27)

The blue sky piece of this life puzzle is submitting to God's control. Alcoholics Anonymous has a saying, "Let go and let God."[18] Letting go is trusting God. It's telling God, "Your will, not mine, be done" (see Matthew 6:10; 26:39). Letting go is realizing that things which came to us when we put ourselves in God's hands are better than anything we could have planned. It's letting go of our preconceived notions of what needs to happen. Letting go and letting God is acknowledging that He is moving history forward regardless of what we do. We go wherever He leads. If God is a current in the river of life, "letting go and letting God" is putting down the paddle and letting the canoe drift.

My husband and I found out what God can do when we let go. We were scheduled to fly from Pakistan to the U.S. with a stopover in Paris. We tried to change our flight to avoid a layover in Frankfurt, but all flights were full for weeks. On our scheduled departure date, we got up early, caught the first train from Colombes and the first metro from the Gare Saint Lazare to Les Invalides. When we arrived at the airport, we learned that our locker had expired. My husband went to pay the extra money and get our locker unlocked while I stood in the long line to check in. Upon reaching the front of the line, still twenty minutes before our flight, we were told that we couldn't get on. We knew there were no other seats out of Paris for weeks, so we did the only thing we could—we put our names on the standby list for a direct flight to New York. We ended up flying first class on a direct flight. Let go and let God. I personally like the idea of pulling up my paddle and going with God. But Jesus also lays out a green tree piece. Instructing His followers to pray and never give up, He told a parable of a widow who kept coming before a judge to plead her case. At first the judge refused her, but after her pestering, he finally said: "Because this widow keeps bothering me, I will see that she gets justice, so that she won't eventually wear me out with her coming!" (Luke 18:1, 5).

We find this green tree piece throughout the Bible. The writer of Ecclesiastes recommends that "a man can do nothing better than to eat and drink and find satisfaction in his work" (2:24). Paul picks up the same argument when he tells the Thessalonians, "We hear that some among you are idle. . . ." (2 Thessalonians 3:11–13). God seems to be telling us to find something to do. Be active!

The green tree piece of the puzzle is the equivalent of *carpe diem*. Seize the day! Seizing opportunities is taking the initiative to make destiny happen. It is living by the proverb "better to have loved and lost than not to have loved at all." It's taking a shot at something when the outcome is unsure. It's grabbing the opportunity to go for the touchdown. It's living by the maxim "opportunity knocks but once."

Rosa Parks seized an opportunity to fight injustice when she refused to give up her bus seat to a white passenger in Montgomery, Alabama, on December 1, 1955. When she was arrested and fined for violating a city ordinance, blacks boycotted the city-owned bus company for 382 days. A Supreme Court decision struck down the Montgomery ordinance, under which Mrs. Parks had been fined, and outlawed racial segregation on public transportation. Her act of defiance was the beginning of the modern civil rights movement in the United States. Mrs. Parks made history in that one moment.

Most of us won't make history, but the opportunities we seize are no less important: teaching at a mission school in Pakistan, bonding with my family climbing Mount Kilimanjaro, snorkeling off the Florida Keys even though I got stung by a Portuguese man-of-war. Paddling my canoe has been deeply satisfying. But we need both sides of this life puzzle.

BLUE SKY PIECE: PASSIVITY

God has a grand plan for all history (and for us in particular) that we can't resist being a part of. "In him we were also chosen, having been predestined according to the plan of him who works out everything in conformity with the purpose of his will" (Ephesians 1:11). And "Being confident of this, that he who began a good work in you will carry it on to completion until the day of Christ Jesus" (Philippians 1:6).

Verses in Proverbs remind us that our lives are ultimately decided by God. "The LORD works out everything for his own ends—even the wicked for a day of disaster" (16:4). "In his heart a man plans his course, but the LORD determines his step" (16:9). "The lot is cast into the lap, but its every decision is from the LORD" (16:33). Isaiah asserts God's ultimate control over history. "The LORD Almighty has sworn, 'Surely, as I have planned, so it will be, and as I have purposed, so it will stand'" (14:24). "For the LORD Almighty has purposed, and who can thwart him? His hand is stretched out, and who can turn it back?" (14:27). An angel broke Peter out of prison the night before he was to stand trial. Peter realized that God rescued him "from Herod's clutches and from everything the Jewish people were anticipating" (Acts 12:11). No plan of Herod's or the Jews could succeed against God's plan. Peter wasn't paddling his canoe that day. He was drifting in the current of God's will.

GREEN TREE PIECE: ACTIVITY

On the *carpe diem* side, we find Jesus complimenting dogged persistence. Praying to God, He said, is like a man going to his friend at midnight to ask for three loaves of bread. The friend eventually got up and gave the man bread because of the man's "shameless audacity" (Luke 11:8). Jesus urges us to do the same.

A non-Jewish woman pleaded with Jesus to heal her demon-possessed daughter. Following Jesus, she kept "crying out" to Him (Matthew 15:23). Jesus tried to send her away. "I was sent only to the lost sheep of Israel," He said, and, "It is not right to take the children's bread and toss it to the dogs" (vv. 24, 26). The woman put her paddle in the water and turned the canoe around when she said to Jesus, "Yes, Lord. But even the dogs eat the crumbs that fall from their masters' table" (v. 27). Impressed by her persistent faith, Jesus healed the woman's daughter.

A wise man gave this advice: "Whatever your hand finds to do, do it with all your might" (Ecclesiastes 9:10). The New Testament counterpart is "Whatever you do, whether in word or deed, do it all in the name of the Lord Jesus" (Colossians 3:17).

PUTTING THE PIECES TOGETHER

Located at the end of the book of Proverbs is the quintessential example of a woman who lives comfortably in the tension of *carpe diem* and "let go and let God." She is, above all things, shrewd and strategic. She creates her own destiny with an ever-present sense of submission to God. She is "a woman who fears the LORD" (Proverbs 31:30).

Shrewdness is having sound judgment, being intuitive, having a gift for discernment, farsightedness, and immunity to deception. The woman of Proverbs 31 is shrewd. She does today what needs to be done so her future will go well. She "selects wool" (v. 13). She is "like merchant ships bringing her food from afar" (v. 14). In other words, she estimates future needs and trades against them. She "provides food" (v. 15) suggesting that she has traded accurately with merchants and has enough food. She "considers" (v. 16). The Hebrew *daman* means to purpose determinedly. Out of the earnings, "she plants a vineyard." She reinvests her capital and thus preserves her investments—contrary to the sluggard who can't be bothered to consume them (Proverbs 12:27, 19:24). She makes sure her trading is profitable and her lamp doesn't go out at night (v. 18). Like the wise virgins in Jesus' parable (Matthew 25:1–13), she has enough oil to keep her lamp burning. Verses 19–20 are arranged chiastically (in an X shape), with the Hebrew word *shalach* ("stretches out") at the beginning of the thought and at the end to make sure the reader sees the connection.

Her hand stretches out (*shalach*) on the distaff

And grasps the spindle with her fingers

She opens her arms to the poor

And extends/stretches out (*shalach*) her hands to the needy.

The chiasm suggests that her shrewdness is related to her ability to share with others. Shrewdness is not taking advantage of people or being greedy. God never encourages greed (Proverbs 15:27; 28:22, 25; Matthew 5:19–24). Shrewdness is thinking ahead so we have enough for ourselves and others. Shrewdness results in having no worry about the future. "When it snows she has no fear" (v. 21). She and her husband are well positioned for the future (vv. 22–23, 25).

How are you shrewd? In the case of career decisions, spend time wisely, learn a skill, take a class, plan ahead, send resumes, and seize opportunities.

IMBALANCE: NOT SEIZING OPPORTUNITIES

We are called to live in the tension between letting God take us where He will and seizing opportunities. Trying to live with one puzzle piece and not the other can result in extremes. Not seizing opportunities is like a football player who stands in the middle of the field and doesn't make any plays. People who don't seize opportunities don't send out resumes; they wait for God to produce jobs out of thin air. They get an early diagnosis of cancer and wait on God instead of getting treatment.

When my husband was in junior high, he was interested in twin girls and wanted to take one to the church social. He called their house and asked to speak to one of the twins. The mother asked which one, and he said it didn't matter. Their mother said, "Well, they really are quite different, you know!" He hung up and never called back. Sometimes we have to seize opportunities.

IMBALANCE: NOT LETTING GO AND LETTING GOD

Those who take *carpe diem* to the extreme fail to acknowledge God's authority and activity and are endlessly busy creating their destiny. They leave nothing to "chance." They pick out their child's preschool, college, and occupation before the child is even born.

James cautions us. He tells us we need to acknowledge God's sovereignty and our own human limitations. "Now listen, you who say, 'Today or tomorrow we will go to this or that city . . .'" (James 4:13–15).

BALANCE: BRINGING IT TOGETHER

Jean de la Fontaine, a French moralist, fit both pieces of this life puzzle together when he wrote, "Help yourself, and heaven will help you."[19] It takes wisdom to live out both puzzle pieces at once. Combining both pieces of the life puzzle results in a partnership: "Continue to work out your salvation with fear and trembling, for it is God who works in you to will and to act according to his good purpose" (Philippians 2:12–13). Proverbs reminds us to "commit to the LORD whatever you do, and your plans will succeed" (16:3). There is an important piece of acknowledging God's sovereignty over history and over us while making plans.

Our pastor canoes with his grandsons. The boys paddle madly and he sits in back and steers the canoe in the right direction. As we paddle, God sits in the back and determines our direction.

WHY CAN'T GOD BE MORE OBVIOUS?

The Proverbs 31 woman demonstrates how to balance "letting go and letting God" with "seizing opportunities." We might wonder why we have to live between these two opposites. We might resent having to paddle when we're unsure whether God is in the back steering. We might resent God not giving us the compass coordinates indicating where we are and where we're going. Resentment might be mixed with desperation. We might desperately want a calling or leading from God so we can have 100 percent certainty about our choices.

I once heard about a woman who prayed every day as to whether or not to vacuum the house. She wanted certainty that she was doing the right thing.

God gives certainty in certain areas. God is particularly concerned about people loving Him and loving others.

Within that love, we are free to select our direction. Paul said, "The only thing that counts is faith expressing itself through love" (Galatians 5:6). Saint Augustine wrote: "Love, and do what you please."[20] Love for God and others drives our choices; the rest is our decision. If vacuuming springs from love of God or others, vacuum. If it doesn't, don't. We don't need additional revelation from God.

FAITH BRINGS CERTAINTY

God seems to indicate that faith gives us certainty. "Now faith is being sure of what we hope for and certain of what we do not see" (Hebrews 11:1). Faith in God gives certainty because our faith is in a person who loves us deeply. "And so we know and rely on the love God has for us. God is love. Whoever lives in love lives in God, and God in him" (1 John 4:16).

Miraculous revelation might be easier, but expecting the miraculous is like expecting God to part a river every time we want to cross to the other side.

Let's take a miracle quiz:

When you come to a river, do you . . .

Pray for God to part the water or to let you walk on water?

Drive over the bridge?

Both?

When you want to pass a test, do you . . .

Pray?

Study?

Both?

When you want to get to work or school on time, do you . . .

Pray?

Set your alarm and leave in good time?

Both?

When you want a boyfriend/girlfriend, do you . . .

Pray?

Go on dates?

Both?

When you want to prevent the black plague or cancer, do you . . .

Pray?

Take steps (get rid of rats; do cancer research)?

Both?

God typically relies on the natural laws that He established at creation. The sun came up this morning, the tides went in and out, and gravity pulled objects toward the center of the earth. It's not that God cannot work outside these laws, but working within them is just as miraculous. Jesus is not in the business of dishing out miracles on demand, and He rebuked the sensationalist desire for miraculous signs: "This is a wicked generation. It asks for a miraculous sign, but none will be given it except the sign of Jonah" (Luke 11:29). In the parable of the rich man and Lazarus, the rich man asks Abraham to send Lazarus to his brothers to tell them what hell is like. Abraham answers: "If they do not listen to Moses and the Prophets, they will not be convinced even if someone rises from the dead" (Luke 16:31). God is looking for people who trust Him by faith apart from miracles that may or may not give us certainty.

As Philip Yancey wrote in his book *Disappointment with God*, "Miracles—dramatic, show-stopping miracles like many of us still long for—simply do not foster deep faith" (p. 117).

THE MIRACLE OF GOD'S LAWS OF NATURE

God set in motion the laws of nature at creation, and He can accomplish His will either by suspending them or by using them. He can miraculously stop the Jordan from flowing or stop the Jordan with a landslide upriver. He can turn water into wine in the blink of an eye or He can use the "natural" process of fermentation. He can create a huge amount of bread in the time it takes to break a few small loaves into pieces or He can use seeds, water, and sunshine to create grain. Men can win battles because the sun stands still or because God joins them in the fight and empowers them to win. He can appear to Paul in a blinding light on the Damascus road or He can speak to us through His Word and the Holy Spirit. He can reveal our career direction through a supernatural appearance, as He did for Isaiah (Isaiah 6), or He can reveal His desires through the natural revelation evident in our skills, values, personality, and interests.

DIRECTION IN OUR GENES

When it comes to big decisions like career and marriage, some of the most helpful information is closer than we think. In fact, some may be surprised to know that God has given us a great deal of direction. He created each of us as unique individuals with unique skills, values, personalities, and interests. Looking at ourselves can increase our *clarity*.

Our youngest son was struggling with a career decision as to whether or not he should go into full-time missions focused on evangelism. He is gifted in math, physics, and computers, and he has a master's of science in electrical engineering. To make his decision he considered his math and computer skills along with his love of helping others solve engineering-type problems. He also considered his own personality, which allows him to sit in front of a computer all day. By taking into account his skills in math and computer science and his passion for missions, he discovered that he didn't have to choose one or the other. He found a "compromise" position working in a mission office overseas helping people with their computers.

Could God have issued a call instead of making our son go through the process of looking at himself? Of course. An unmistakable call from God would have given our son more certainty. But waiting for this kind of supernatural call is like looking for a second revelation when He has already revealed Himself.

The story is told of a man caught in a flood who was standing on his roof waiting for God to intervene and save him. A rescue boat came by, but he refused the help. "God is going to rescue me," he said. Then men in a helicopter tried to rescue him, but again the man refused. "God is going to rescue me," he said again. Finally he drowned, went to heaven, and asked God why He didn't rescue him. God answered, "I sent a boat and a helicopter."

Sometimes we wait for God's miraculous intervention when He is using natural means to meet our needs. We wait for the supernatural call when He has already called us "naturally" in His creation of our skills, values, personality, and interests.

THE CALL OF GOD

A moving documentary[21] about five women who served as medical missionaries in Pakistan describes how each one chose to give up the privileges of life in North America, the possibility of successful careers, the respect they would have enjoyed, and their own possibilities for marriage and family life. They all said the same thing: they felt the call of God on their lives. What does that mean?

A calling is a growing sense about the truth of an idea. It happens when we feel an irrepressible desire to follow God in a certain direction. Call can be subtle. But it can happen. It is the sense that the river current is getting stronger and carrying us in a certain direction. How does this happen?

THE HOLY SPIRIT LEADS US

Paul began to follow Jesus after being stopped by a blinding light and hearing the voice of the Lord while on his way to Damascus (Acts 9:3–6). The Lord then appeared to him in a vision, and he began preaching. Later in Acts we read: "The Holy Spirit said: 'Set apart for me Barnabas and Saul for the work to which I have called them'" (13:2). Paul continued to see visions (Acts 16:9) and make decisions based on the Holy Spirit's nudging: "Compelled by the Spirit, I am going to Jerusalem, not knowing what will happen to me there" (Acts 20:22).

Paul also made decisions based on information. Paul decided to go to Jerusalem "after all this had happened" (Acts 19:21). "Because the Jews made a plot against him just as he was about to sail for Syria, he decided to go back through Macedonia" (Acts 20:3). He made his decision based on what was happening.

But how do we know that our decisions are the right ones? We have no guarantees. Waiting for that guarantee from God is like waiting for a guarantee from a grocery store that the melon we're buying will be sweet. We can smell the melon and thump it all we want, but to really know if the melon is good, we have to eat it. Sometimes, knowing God's will for our life will involve "smelling out and thumping" the new direction, and then moving ahead with some uncertainty.

DISCERNMENT GROUPS

In the Quaker tradition, "discernment groups" help a person determine whether a call is really from God. The group asks pointed questions, considers facts, and listens for God's will to emerge through the consensus of the group. While some Quakers convene formal discernment groups,[22] some convene informal groups of friends and family. Sometimes the Holy Spirit directs us through the input of others.

WHAT KIND OF PUZZLE IS THIS?

When making decisions, we need to strike a balance between the extremes of being passive and active. We paddle while acknowledging that God is in the back of our canoe setting the direction. We acknowledge God's control over our lives and seize opportunity. We act shrewdly while at the same time submitting ourselves to God's will. We look at our skills, values, and personalities while listening to the Holy Spirit's special leading. We partner with God in working out our salvation and looking for His working in our lives. What kind of puzzle is this? The blue sky and green tree pieces are true at all times. At all times we need to move forward while relying on God to direct us according to His sovereign will.

QUESTIONS FOR GROUP DISCUSSION OR PERSONAL REFLECTION

- How has God led you in the past? How do you expect Him to lead you in the future?

- How do you achieve certainty in your decision making?

- How do you balance waiting on God's sovereignty and moving forward?

- What has God revealed to you through your skills, values, and personality? What has God revealed to you through the Spirit's leading?

GOD'S GLORY

In Strength or in Weakness?

BLUE SKY

"My grace is sufficient for you, for my power is made perfect in weakness." (2 Corinthians 12:9)

I can do everything through him who gives me strength. (Philippians 4:13)

GREEN TREE

If the whole body were an eye, where would the sense of hearing be? If the whole body were an ear, where would the sense of smell be? But in fact God has arranged the parts in the body, every one of them, just as he wanted them to be. If they were all one part, where would the body be? (1 Corinthians 12:17–19)

We have different gifts. (Romans 12:6)

COUNSELOR & CLIENT CONVERSATION

ME: Have you thought about making a career decision based on your strengths, your gifts?

CAROL: I'm not sure I have gifts. But if I do, I think God will get the most glory if He uses my weaknesses.

ME: How does that work?

CAROL: Well, if I use my strengths everyone will know it's me doing the great things. But if I use my weaknesses everyone will know that God deserves the credit.

ME: So He prefers to use your weaknesses?

CAROL: Definitely. The Bible says so.

ME: Why did He give you strengths and gifts?

CAROL: I don't know. But if I use them, I'll get a big head.

ME: How do you know that?

CAROL: My mom told me.

ME: So using your weaknesses gives glory to God and using your strengths gives glory to you.

CAROL: Yes.

GOD CREATED EACH OF US UNIQUELY. THE ODDS of someone else having our unique biological makeup are less than 1 out of 70 trillion. We are as different from each other as a water pitcher and a butter dish.

Comparing ourselves to dishes isn't far off the mark. The prophet Isaiah wrote: "Yet, O LORD, you are our Father. We are the clay, you are the potter; we are all the work of your hand" (64:8). This is a wonderful comparison. As a potter intentionally and uniquely shapes each pot for a certain purpose, so God intentionally and uniquely shapes us for specific tasks.

STRENGTHS FOR DIFFERENT TASKS

Jesus and Paul both spoke about different tasks involved in building the church. Jesus spoke about sowers and reapers:

> "The saying 'One sows and another reaps' is true. I sent you to reap what you have not worked for. Others have done the hard work, and you have reaped the benefits of their labor." (John 4:37)

Paul mentioned planters and waterers:

> "What, after all, is Apollos? And what is Paul? Only servants, through whom you came to believe—as the Lord has assigned to each his task. I planted the seed,

Apollos watered it, but God made it grow."
(1 Corinthians 3:5–6)

One of our tasks in life is to find and develop our strengths and gifts, faithfully offer them to God, and wait on Him for the results. That's the green tree piece of the puzzle.

However, there are some people, like my client, who believe that God wants us to focus on our weaknesses. Others have strengths they're afraid to acknowledge. That's the blue sky piece of the puzzle.

A butter dish is perfect for serving butter but not for pouring water. Why don't we use a butter dish to pour water into glasses? It's not the right shape. It wasn't created for pouring water. A water pitcher is perfect for pouring water but not for serving butter. Why don't we use a water pitcher to serve butter? It's not the right shape. It wasn't created for serving butter. The same is true for humans. We are different shapes, and our different shapes give us different strengths for accomplishing different tasks.

In addition, when we became Christians God gave us special gifts. "Each man has his own gift from God" (1 Corinthians 7:7). No ifs, ands, or buts, you are uniquely created with strengths and gifts.

Because of these different gifts, each Christian plays a unique part in establishing Christ's kingdom here on earth. Paul emphasized the importance of all Christians using their giftedness when he wrote:

> If the whole body were an eye, where would the sense of hearing be? If the whole

> body were an ear, where would the sense
> of smell be? But in fact God has arranged
> the parts in the body, every one of them,
> just as he wanted them to be. If they were
> all one part, where would the body be? As
> it is, there are many parts, but one body.
> (1 Corinthians 12:17–20)

Does a pot or dish bring glory to its maker by serving its purpose or some other purpose? I'm definitely more impressed with a pitcher that holds water than one that leaks. But some Christians have the notion that God's strength is more visible when they try to do something in their area of weakness rather than their strength. They quote Paul who said, "I can do everything through [the Lord] who gives me strength" (Philippians 4:13) as if it means they should try to be something they're not.

Do you run into more red lights when you're late or when you're early? It sure seems as if I have to stop for more red lights when I'm late. Is it because there are more red lights or because I'm more aware of them? Perceptions change depending on our circumstances. The same is true of our sense that we experience more of God's strength when we operate from a place of weakness. He strengthens us all the time, but we're more aware of it during times of weakness.

> So do not fear, for I am with you; do not be
> dismayed, for I am your God. I will strengthen
> you and help you; I will uphold you with my
> righteous right hand. (Isaiah 41:10)

God strengthens us when we feel weak *and* when we feel strong. The apostle Paul discovered God's strength in all kinds of circumstances:

> I have learned to be content whatever the circumstances. I know what it is to be in need, and I know what it is to have plenty. I have learned the secret of being content in any and every situation, whether well fed or hungry, whether living in plenty or in want. I can do everything through him who gives me strength." (Philippians 4:11–13)

God's strength was available to Paul when he was in need and when he was hungry. But God's strength was also available to him when he had plenty and when he was well fed. But like red lights when we're late, we may notice His presence more clearly when we're in trouble.

God is with us at all times, not only when we feel weak. However, we feel God's strength more often during weakness because we're more aware of our need for it, not because it's God's will for us to remain weak.

Another passage that causes some Christians to think God receives more glory when they focus on their weaknesses is found in 2 Corinthians. Paul wrote: "My grace is sufficient for you, for my power is made perfect in weakness" (12:9–10).

In this letter Paul is defending his apostleship to the Corinthian church.

The Corinthians had a list of what they liked and didn't like in evangelists. They liked flash and pizzazz. Paul said, "You are looking only on the surface of things" (2 Corinthians 10:7).

Paul apparently didn't have flash and pizzazz and thus looked weak to them. In response he wrote: "For some say, 'His letters are weighty and forceful, but in person he is unimpressive and his speaking amounts to nothing'" (2 Corinthians 10:10).

Paul didn't think of himself as weak at all. "But I do not think I am in the least inferior to those "super-apostles" (2 Corinthians 11:5). Compared to them, he had important strengths:

- Knowledge (11:5).
- Humility—he lowered himself to elevate Corinthian believers (v. 7).
- Lineage—he was a Hebrew, an Israelite, and a descendant of Abraham (v. 22)
- Apostolic commitment—he had worked harder than any other apostle, been in prison more frequently, been flogged more severely, and been exposed to death repeatedly (23–28).

In addition, he had been "caught up" into heaven where he heard "inexpressible" things (2 Corinthians 12:4). These strengths could have made him conceited, but they didn't because Paul also was given a thorn in the flesh: "To keep me from becoming conceited because of these surpassingly great revelations, there was given me a thorn in my flesh, a messenger of Satan, to torment me" (2 Corinthians 12:7).

Paul understood God's purpose for weakness: "That is why, for Christ's sake, I delight in weaknesses, in insults, in hardships, in persecutions, in difficulties" (2 Corinthians 12:10). The Greek word translated "weakness" is *astheneia* and refers to the weakness felt when you're ill or when you don't feel up to the tasks of life.

The positive side of such weaknesses is that God's "grace is sufficient for you for [His] power is made perfect in weakness" (2 Corinthians 12:9). The word "perfect" (*teleo* in Greek) means "to complete or finish." This is the same root word found in John 19:30 when Jesus said, "It is finished." Paul was saying that God's power finds its completion in the presence of personal weakness and challenging situations.

The summary of the argument is that Paul says he is just as good or better than super apostles because God's power is made complete in the presence of his weaknesses.

These verses do not suggest that we should ignore our strengths and try to be a water pitcher if we were created to be a butter dish. They suggest that although we have strengths, we also have weaknesses that God powerfully completes. The purpose of Paul's thorn was to prevent conceit. But the purpose of strengths and gifts is to establish God's kingdom on earth. Paul doesn't contradict the concept that each Christian must operate from his or her place of giftedness for the body to run as it should.

Over and over in the Bible, we witness how God takes our insufficient offerings and uses them for amazing purposes.

This is what happened with the young boy who offered his lunch to Jesus (John 6:1–15). Five loaves and two fish is a pretty good lunch for a little guy, but the boy and his lunch were "weak" in that they could not feed 5,000 people. God's power found its completion in the presence of this "weakness" resulting in twelve baskets of leftovers.

When our youngest son was ten, he wasn't good at catching the football but he was good enough at throwing it. One day during a neighborhood pick-up game, my husband said to our son, "Just throw it as hard as you can." My husband caught what our son threw and ran it for a touchdown. That's what God does for us. He takes what we have to offer in improbably difficult situations and scores the touchdowns.

David in the face of Goliath had weaknesses. He was inexperienced at war. He had never worn armor. He was young and his brother thought he was conceited (1 Samuel 17:28). His strengths were his fearlessness, his faith in the God of Israel, and his skill with a slingshot. These did not seem like strengths in the face of nine-foot Goliath (1 Samuel 17). But David chose to face Goliath with his strength (his slingshot) and not with his weakness (his inexperience with armor). God got the victory that day, not because David focused on his weakness but because he trusted God to do something with his strength.

HEBREWS 11: THE HALL OF STRENGTHS AND WEAKNESSES

Have you seen a football player make a touchdown and give the glory to God by pointing an index finger skyward? That's what Hebrews 11 does with its examples of people using their weaknesses and their strengths. At the end of the chapter is this summary:

> And what more shall I say? I do not have time to tell about Gideon, Barak, Samson, Jephthah, David, Samuel and the prophets, who through faith . . . escaped the edge of the sword; whose weakness was turned to strength; and who became powerful in battle and routed foreign armies. (Hebrews 11:32)

Gideon was a reluctant leader, but is called "mighty warrior" by the angel of God (Judges 6:12). He is described as having "the bearing of a prince" (Judges 8:18). Barak, though reluctant, was willing to go to battle if Deborah, the prophetess, went along. He is mentioned as a man of faith because he believed that with God and Deborah, he would win (Judges 4). Samson's asset was God-given strength (Judges 13:5). "Jephthah the Gileadite was a mighty warrior" (Judges 11:1). David was described to Saul as someone "who knows how to play the harp. He is a brave man and a warrior. He speaks well and is a fine-looking man. And the LORD is with him" (1 Samuel 16:18).

These men all had a God-given strength to be used for God-ordained purposes.

But they also had weaknesses. Gideon didn't want to go up against the Midianites because he was from a small clan and was "the least" in his family (Judges 6:15). Barak was afraid to go up against the Canaanites without Deborah, the prophetess (Judges 4:8). Samson was susceptible to women (Judges 14:16–17; 16:17). Jephthah, the illegitimate son of a prostitute, was driven from the family by his mother's legitimate sons (Judges 11:2). David was a simple shepherd boy. His oldest brother mocked him and accused him of being wicked and conceited: "Why have you come down here? And with whom did you leave those few sheep in the desert? I know how conceited you are and how wicked your heart is; you came down only to watch the battle" (1 Samuel 17:28).

GOD USES STRENGTHS AND WEAKNESSES

These people show up in Hebrews 11 because they had faith that God would use their strengths and their weaknesses. We see this over and over in the Bible. People in the Bible who struggled with weakness also had basic strengths. Despite statements of weakness, these individuals suffered more from crises of confidence than competency.

God chose Mary to be the mother of His Son because of her humility. Most people don't recognize humility as strength, but Mary was willing to put up with the shame of being an unwed mother for the glory of God. After being chosen for this sacred purpose, Mary said, "He has been mindful of the humble state of his servant. From now on all generations will call me blessed" (Luke 1:48).

In *The Purpose Driven Life*, Rick Warren quotes a Danish

proverb: "What you are is God's gift to you; what you do is your gift to God."

WHY DOESN'T GOD CHANGE MY WEAKNESSES INTO STRENGTHS?

If God chose to do so, He could give me the ability to design a house or write a song or lead worship in church. He could have made food for 5,000 people out of nothing instead of multiplying the five loaves and two fish given to him by a young boy. He could have given David the ability to carry the armor into battle with Goliath. But for the most part, God uses what He already created. Though God can turn my weaknesses into strengths, He seems to use my strengths and complete my weaknesses.

WHAT IS FAITH?

Sometimes we make decisions as if faith is trusting God to use our weakness. We consider it an act of faith to do a job we're not prepared for or suited for. But faith is trusting God in my strengths and in my weaknesses. Faith is using what I am and have for God and trusting Him for the outcome. Faith is based on our knowledge of God and ourselves. The psalmist says that faith in God saves an army, but warriors still show up for battle with armor and horses.

> No king is saved by the size of his army;
> no warrior escapes by his great strength.
> A horse is a vain hope for deliverance;
> despite all its great strength it cannot save.

> But the eyes of the LORD are on those who
> fear him, on those whose hope is in his
> unfailing love. (Psalm 33:16–18)

Even though David recognized God's preeminent role
in a victory, he didn't go to battle without an army.

WHAT ABOUT CONCEIT?

Some parents never compliment their children's strengths
due to fear of making them think too highly of themselves.
However, we don't get conceited over our strengths when we
know they are a gift from God and that He is responsible for
any success that comes from using them.

> What, after all, is Apollos? And what is
> Paul? Only servants, through whom you
> came to believe—as the Lord has assigned
> to each his task. I planted the seed, Apollos
> watered it, but God made it grow. So
> neither he who plants nor he who waters is
> anything, but only God, who makes things
> grow. (1 Corinthians 3:5–6)

Twelve baskets of leftovers made it clear that God,
not the young boy, was the hero of the day. When David
triumphed over Goliath, David made it clear that God was
the hero: "It is not by sword or spear that the LORD saves
[or by sling shot!]; for the battle is the LORD's" (1 Samuel
17:47).

In each Hebrews 11 narrative, God is credited as the reason for the victory. Each man of faith knew the source of his success. Where is each man's weakness in these narratives? They knew that apart from God they were too weak to accomplish what needed to be done. Their strength alone was insufficient. The men knew that no matter how well prepared they were, the outcome was up to God.

Faith is trusting God for the outcome. We prepare ourselves as much as we can, and we leave the outcome to God.

> It was not by their sword that they won the land, nor did their arm bring them victory; it was your right hand, your arm, and the light of your face, for you loved them. You are my King and my God, who decrees victories for Jacob. Through you we push back our enemies; through your name we trample our foes. I do not trust in my bow, my sword does not bring me victory; but you give us victory over our enemies, you put our adversaries to shame. In God we make our boast all day long, and we will praise your name forever. (Psalm 44:3–8)

God does His part and we do ours. He is responsible for the ultimate outcome, and we give Him the credit. Even when we operate from our place of strengths and giftedness, God deserves the glory. To put these puzzle pieces together requires that we use our strengths and trust God to complete our weakness.

PUZZLE TYPE

We started out thinking that God wanted to use our weaknesses in some miraculous way and avoid using our strength to avoid pride. But now we see how strength and weakness fit together in the puzzle. We have weaknesses. We have strengths. We don't deny either. We use both for God's glory at all times.

QUESTIONS FOR GROUP DISCUSSION OR PERSONAL REFLECTION

- What are some of your strengths? If you aren't aware of your strengths, how can you go about finding them? How can you develop your strengths?

- What are some of your weaknesses?

- How has God used some of your strengths?

- How has God used some of your weaknesses?

- What is God's response when we don't use the strengths He gave us?

MY MIND
Flesh or Spirit?

BLUE SKY

While they were going out, a man who was demon-possessed and could not talk was brought to Jesus. And when the demon was driven out, the man who had been mute spoke. (Matthew 9:32–33)

GREEN TREE

[T]wo blind men followed [Jesus], calling out, "Have mercy on us, Son of David!" When he had gone indoors, the blind men came to him, and he asked them, "Do you believe that I am able to do this?" "Yes, Lord," they replied. Then he touched their eyes and said, "According to your faith will it be done to you"; and their sight was restored. (Matthew 9:27–30)

"There was given me a thorn in my flesh, a messenger of Satan, to torment me." (2 Corinthians 12:7)

"Stop drinking only water, and use a little wine because of your stomach and your frequent illnesses." (1 Timothy 5:23)

COUNSELOR & CLIENT CONVERSATION

CAROL: When I feel like a failure, I feel depressed. And then I feel like a double failure, because I'm a failure and I'm depressed.

ME: So feeling depressed makes you feel like a failure?

CAROL: Yes, I don't think Christians are supposed to feel down.

ME: Why aren't Christians supposed to feel down?

CAROL: Well, because if you pray enough to God, you should feel joyful in every circumstance.

ME: And that means you can't feel down?

CAROL: That's right.

ME: Do you think any of the people in the Bible ever felt down?

CAROL: Yes, but that was a sin!

ME: So feeling depressed is always a sin. Depression is a spiritual weakness. And not being depressed means that you're a strong Christian.

CAROL: Well, I don't know about "strong." But good Christians don't get depressed, period.

YESTERDAY THE LAMP ON MY DESK STOPPED working. My theory was that the light bulb was loose. I tried tightening the bulb, but it was already tight. So my loose bulb theory didn't fit the situation. I had to develop another theory. I checked other lights in the room. They were working, so the theory that the electricity was off in the house didn't fit. I finally realized that no electricity was getting to my lamp because I had stepped on the surge protector and turned it off. Once I figured out the cause, I knew the solution.

Theories are useful because they propose two things: the cause of the problem and the cure.

Finding the cause and the cure to a lamp malfunction does not rank high on the list of serious matters. But what do we do when the situation is more serious?

When our second son was ten years old, he contracted meningitis. He was hospitalized, treated, and discharged. But he became sick again just as we were returning for his follow-up appointment. The pediatrician theorized that our son was worried about coming back to the doctor's office. But our son's condition was much more serious than anxiety about a doctor's visit. We learned that meningitis can be "bimodal," meaning that it recurs. Finding the cause for the second occurrence of meningitis was important so that we could apply the right cure. If our son had been upset by doctors' visits, we would have comforted him. But what happens when we can't identify the cause or cure? Humans fear situations without known causes or cures.

During the Middle Ages, humans feared the Black Plague. The epidemic swept across Europe in the fourteenth century causing widespread hysteria because no one knew the cause or the cure. People tried all manner of cures, including quarantine, wearing herbs, and bloodletting.[23,] One group, known as the Flagellants,[24] speculated that the cause was spiritual and came up with a spiritual cure. The Flagellants wandered in bands through towns and countryside doing penance in public.[25] Flagellants would flog their shoulders and arms with iron points and draw their own blood. They believed that public penance would atone for the evil of the world and the plague would stop. In October 1349, the Pope condemned them and ordered authorities to stop them.

We might feel shocked at these Flagellants today. They were trying to solve a flea problem spiritually. They believed that problems, especially ones they didn't understand, were spiritually caused and spiritually solved.

CHRISTIANS HAVE MENTAL HEALTH PROBLEMS

Some Christians have a theory that mental health problems are caused by spiritual weakness. They speculate that Christians who are following God are immune from mental health problems. Therefore, Christians who experience mental health problems are spiritually weak or not real Christians.[26]

However, this theory doesn't fit reality. At any point in time, one out of five Americans has a mental health problem. That's about 20 percent of the population.[27] And some of these are Christians. I've worked with Christians who struggle with all types of mental health problems, including depression, anxiety, and psychotic illnesses like schizophrenia. Some of them have a strong relationship with God, yet they still suffer from mental health problems.

MENTAL HEALTH PROBLEMS MAY NOT IMPROVE WITH SPIRITUAL INTERVENTION ONLY

Those who speculate that the cause and cure of all mental health problems is spiritual are doing the same thing as Flagellants. When my husband and I were having marriage problems, we went to see a pastor. His solution was for us to become Christians. But we already were Christians. So we felt more confused as to why we couldn't get marriage right. The message we heard was that "real" Christians don't have marriage problems. This pastor's theory did not allow any other explanations or solutions.

SOME ILLNESS IS SPIRITUALLY CAUSED

Some health problems *do* have a spiritual cause. Sometimes Satan possesses or oppresses people and they get sick. We know that "Satan went out from the presence of the LORD and afflicted Job with painful sores from the soles of his feet to the top of his head" (Job 2:7). Satan can cause illness. Paul's thorn in the flesh was a messenger of Satan: "There was given me a thorn in my flesh, a messenger of Satan, to torment me" (2 Corinthians 12:7). Evil spirits can cause torment: "Now the Spirit of the LORD had departed from Saul, and an evil [or harmful] spirit from the LORD tormented him" (1 Samuel 16:14). This demon caused

Saul such torment that he even tried to kill David: "But an evil [or harmful] spirit from the LORD came upon Saul as he was sitting in his house with his spear in his hand. While David was playing the harp, Saul tried to pin him to the wall with his spear, but David eluded him" (1 Samuel 19:9–10). Demons can cause physical problems. Jesus healed muteness by casting out a demon: "While they were going out, a man who was demon-possessed and could not talk was brought to Jesus. And when the demon was driven out, the man who had been mute spoke" (Matthew 9:32–33).

BLUE SKY AND GREEN TREE PIECES

Some passages in the Bible are the blue sky piece of this puzzle: health problems are spiritually caused and cured. Other Bible passages represent the green tree piece: some health problems are physically caused and cured. In contrast to the blue sky passages we just looked at, we find some surprising green tree pieces.

JESUS HEALED WITHOUT CASTING OUT DEMONS

Before Jesus healed the demon-possessed mute, He healed two blind men without casting out demons.

> As Jesus went on from there, two blind men followed him, calling out, "Have mercy on us, Son of David!" When he had gone indoors, the blind men came to him,

> and he asked them, "Do you believe that
> I am able to do this?" "Yes, Lord," they
> replied. Then he touched their eyes and
> said, "According to your faith will it be
> done to you"; and their sight was restored.
> (Matthew 9:27–30)

The two blind men's spiritual faith was important for
their miraculous healing, but Jesus didn't attribute the
cause to a spiritual problem like demon-possession or sin.
Earlier, Jesus healed a woman who had been bleeding for
many years.

> Just then a woman who had been subject
> to bleeding for twelve years came up
> behind him and touched the edge of his
> cloak. She said to herself, "If I only touch
> his cloak, I will be healed." Jesus turned
> and saw her. "Take heart, daughter," he
> said, "your faith has healed you." And the
> woman was healed from that moment.
> (Matthew 9:20–22)

Jesus' disciples tried to assign a spiritual cause—sin—
to a man's blindness, but Jesus disagreed.

> As he went along, [Jesus] saw a man blind
> from birth. His disciples asked him, "Rabbi,
> who sinned, this man or his parents, that
> he was born blind?" "Neither this man nor

his parents sinned," said Jesus, "but this
happened so that the work of God might
be displayed in his life." (John 9:1–3)

Jesus treated some illnesses differently—without
applying a spiritual cause or cure. So did Paul. He told
Timothy, "Stop drinking only water, and use a little wine
because of your stomach and your frequent illnesses"
(1 Timothy 5:23). Paul didn't tell Timothy to pray more.
Paul didn't speculate as to a spiritual cause for Timothy's
health problem. He proposed a physical rather than a
spiritual solution.

PHYSICAL BASES OF MENTAL HEALTH PROBLEMS

The cause of mental health problems is little understood
by the public, but the medical community has made great
progress in its understanding. Mental health problems often
are as much physical illnesses as the flu or diabetes, and they
sometimes require physical interventions. Dr. Otto Loewi[28]
with Sir Henry Dale received the Nobel Prize in 1936 for
discovering chemicals in the brain called neurotransmitters.
These chemicals transmit information from one neuron
to the next. People with certain mental health problems
have too many or too few of these neurotransmitters.
Scientists have also found medicines that help to correct
the imbalances.

Talk therapy can also help change neurotransmitter
imbalances and can help people gain skills that enable them
to recover from mental health problems. A combination

of medicine and talk therapy results in more permanent mental health improvement and is recommended for treatment of mental health problems like major depression. The scientific evidence argues for a physical cause and intervention.

EMOTIONS OF SPIRITUALLY STRONG INDIVIDUALS

Spiritually strong individuals also experience strong emotions. Some Christians categorize emotions as "good" or "bad." Christians feel okay with "good emotions," like contentment and joy, but not with "bad emotions," like sadness, anger, or worry. They believe "bad" emotions reflect a lack of faith in God.

Jesus may have felt "bad" emotions when He entered the temple courts and "drove out all who were buying and selling there. He overturned the tables of the moneychangers" (Matthew 21:12). In the garden before His arrest, He said, "My soul is overwhelmed with sorrow to the point of death" (Matthew 26:38). Despite His faith in God the Father, Jesus felt overwhelming sorrow. Elijah felt overwhelmed to the point of death as well. In fact, when he was running for his life from Jezebel, queen of Israel, he might even have felt suicidal.

> Elijah was afraid and ran for his life. When he came to Beersheba in Judah, he left his servant there, while he himself went a day's journey into the desert. He came to a broom tree, sat down under it and prayed that he

might die. "I have had enough, LORD," he
said. "Take my life; I am no better than my
ancestors." (1 Kings 19:3–4)

Lamentations captures Jeremiah's despair after Judah
went into exile. Chapter one describes emotions like
bitterness and betrayal (v. 2), affliction and distress (v. 3),
grief and bitter anguish (v. 4). Jeremiah grieved deeply
despite his hope in God.

My soul is downcast within me. Yet this
I call to mind and therefore I have hope:
Because of the LORD's great love we are not
consumed, for his compassions never fail.
(Lamentations 3:20–22)

Jesus said that we should not worry (Matthew 6:25–34),
and Peter quoted a psalm of David when he advised young
men and elders to "cast all your anxiety on him" (1 Peter
5:7; Psalm 55:22). Faith in God can alleviate worry and
help us manage anxiety. Yet Paul admitted feeling anxious:
"Therefore I am all the more eager to send him, so that
when you see him again you may be glad and I may have
less anxiety" (Philippians 2:28).

The Psalms capture soul-deep emotional struggles of
spiritual people: "My soul is weary with sorrow," wrote
David (Psalm 119:28).

Psalm 102, introduced as "A prayer of an afflicted
man. When he is faint and pours out his lament before
the LORD," describes physical and emotional struggles as

the author aligns his soul with his spiritual experience of God. God seems to honor his struggle. Just as Christians are not immune to colds, diabetes, and cancer, they are not immune to "bad emotions."

THE PROBLEM WITH ONLY ONE PIECE

If we accept only the green tree piece of the puzzle—that mental health problems are physically caused and cured—does it mean that Christians shouldn't pray or trust God when they are suffering from mental health problems? If we accept only the blue sky piece of the puzzle—that mental health problems are spiritually caused and cured—does it mean that Christians shouldn't make use of available science and medicine?

WHY THE GREEN TREE PIECE IS NOT ENOUGH

If mental health problems are physically caused and cured, do Christians need to pray and trust God when suffering a mental health problem? Of course. We are told to "pray continually" (1 Thessalonians 5:17) and to "trust in [God] at all times" (Psalm 62:8). We pray because we're commanded to do so, and because we have a spirit. Humans are incredibly complex. We have many sides, including a spiritual side, a psychological side, and a physical side. These are called "spirit," "soul," and "body." Paul said, "May your whole spirit, soul and body be kept blameless at the coming of our Lord Jesus Christ" (1 Thessalonians 5:23). We pray every day because we have a spiritual side that needs to be nourished for now and for eternity. We eat every day because we have a body that needs to be fed. We refresh our psychological side every day because we have a soul that needs to be taken care of. We care for each part of ourselves to prevent one or more of the parts from breaking down or getting diseased.

We also pray because our spiritual side helps us through tough times. The psalmist said that his relationship with God helped him when he was anxious: "When anxiety was great within me, your consolation brought joy to my soul" (Psalm 94:19).

Even science tells us that prayer reduces stress and contributes to health.[29]

BOTH SPIRITUAL AND PSYCHOLOGICAL

Instead of either spiritual or physical, we integrate the two. I once worked with a very anxious client who had been severely abused by a male authority figure. Her experience made it difficult for her to trust God. We worked through her sense of threat around male figures with therapy and medications, prescribed by a physician, and we discussed how her experience affected her spiritually. The mental health problem overlapped with the spiritual problem.

WHY THE BLUE SKY PIECE IS NOT ENOUGH

The Flagellants believed that physical illness (e.g., the plague) was spiritually caused and cured. The Christian Science cult is similar. In this tradition, treatment involves spiritual healing in the form of prayer and opening the person's thoughts to the laws of God that maintain health. It does not include seeking treatment from doctors.

As Christians, we disagree with practitioners of Christian Science when it comes to physical illness, but some agree when it comes to mental health problems. When Christians are physically ill, they pray and trust God, but they also seek medical treatment for their condition. When it comes to physical illness, Christians agree that some illnesses are physically caused and cured.

Recently my dad was diagnosed with diabetes. He controls it by healthy eating. But what if he decided only to pray about it and not to change his diet? Would that be a good idea? Or would it be irresponsible to not take advantage of modern medical knowledge?

IS IT ANY DIFFERENT WITH MENTAL HEALTH PROBLEMS?

If a bear attacked, we'd fight it with pepper spray or sticks and rocks. If bees were attacking a baby, we'd do more than pray. If bacteria were attacking a child, we'd take the child to the doctor for antibiotics. If hormone levels dropped after giving birth and triggered postpartum depression, we'd get treatment from our doctor. If neurotransmitters are out of balance, should we do more than pray?

WHY THE BLUE SKY PIECE IS NOT ENOUGH FOR MENTAL HEALTH PROBLEMS

Since Jesus did not ascribe a spiritual cause (like demon

possession) or solution (like exorcism) to all physical health problems, and since some mental health problems have a biological basis, we cannot assume that all mental health problems are spiritually caused and cured. Furthermore, ascribing spiritual causes and cures to all mental health issues can have spiritually devastating effects. I once worked with a woman suffering from depression. Her church held an exorcism for her. Afterward she was still depressed and vowed never to return to the church.

When spiritual interventions fail to cure biologically based mental health problems, Christians are left feeling like spiritual failures. They wonder why prayer doesn't work. They wonder if they're not praying properly. They wonder if some sin is preventing them from being healed psychologically. They wonder if God would heal them if only they were better Christians. They feel let down by God who should "hear from heaven and . . . heal" (2 Chronicles 7:14). And some stop going to church.

We need to understand that although God is the great physician who can heal all our infirmities, He sometimes chooses not to heal us miraculously even if we are righteous like Job. Just as prayer alone sometimes does not heal the black plague or diabetes, sometimes prayer alone does not regulate neurotransmitters.

Of course, God can answer our prayer and heal miraculously. God can cure my father's diabetes. God can reverse heart disease without the help of modern medicine. God can also cause medicines to work faster than they would without His miraculous intervention. James addressed this issue. He told the elders of the church to pray for the sick and anoint them with oil. Oil was a well-known ancient medicine mentioned in the parable of the good samaritan (Luke 10:34). James also told the sick to ask for forgiveness for their sins if sin was present.

> Is any one of you sick? He should call the elders of the church to pray over him and anoint him with oil in the name of the Lord. And the prayer offered in faith will make the sick person well; the Lord will raise him up. If he has sinned, he will be forgiven. Therefore confess your sins to each other and pray for each other so that you may be healed. The prayer of a righteous man is powerful and effective. (James 5:14–16)

We all know instances in which God has chosen to heal miraculously and instances in which He has chosen not to. James' point is that prayer is powerful and we should ask for healing. James recognizes that all healing ultimately comes from God.

WHY WE NEED SCIENCE

In addition to prayer, we also seek the best medicine available. If healing ultimately comes from God, why seek medicines or therapy? Because when God gave humans dominion over the earth (Genesis 1:28), He asked us to "rule over every living creature that moves on the ground," including humans. Through science, we observe humans and find out how they "work." The science of medicine observes disease so that it can be prevented, diagnosed, and treated. The science of psychology observes human behavior so that psychopathology can be prevented, diagnosed, and treated. Through science, we learn truth that isn't in the Bible. Although the Bible is all true, the Bible does not contain all truth. This is how Dr. Arthur Holmes put it:

> To say that all truth is God's truth does not mean that all truth is either contained in the Bible or deducible from what we find there. Historic Christianity has believed in the truthfulness of Scripture, yet not as an exhaustive revelation of everything men can know or want to know as true, but rather as a sufficient rule for faith and conduct.[30]

For example, Jesus told the disciples to "go and make disciples of all nations" (Matthew 28:19), but He didn't explain how to build ships to take them there. The Bible says, "Above all else, guard your heart, for it is the wellspring of life" (Proverbs 4:23). But it is from the science of psychology that we have learned about the human tendency to search for or interpret information in a way that confirms our preconceptions. The Bible is God's gift of inspired revelation telling us how to be in a relationship with Him and others, but not a manual on how to subdue the earth. The Bible has a lot to say about avoiding temptation but not how subliminal messaging is processed by the brain and how that processing affects temptation. The Bible has a lot to say about practicing the disciplines of prayer and forgiveness and provides a basis for motivation to change, but psychology fleshes out more completely the stages that people go through before making a change.

WHY WE NEED THE BIBLE

Some might be concerned that discovery of some truth outside the Bible is a criticism of the Bible. It is not. The Bible says of itself that it is "useful for teaching, rebuking, correcting and training in righteousness" so that we may be "thoroughly equipped for every good work" (2 Timothy 3:16–17).

In the Bible, we find what we need to refresh our spirits. The Bible reveals the truths that feed our hungry and tired souls. It is not through science but through God's inspired Word that we learn about God who created us in His image. We learn that we became sinners through Satan's temptation. In reading the Bible, we learn that our Creator loved us so much that He provided the means to forgive our sin—He sent His Son, Jesus, to be born as an infant, to be crucified on our behalf, and to rise from the dead on the third day. Psychology provides us with much important information, but it does not provide us with the ultimate truths. Without the Bible, we wouldn't know that God loves us or how to love God, others, and ourselves. We wouldn't know about our ultimate destiny or our purpose. We learn in the Bible that God controls history and that He will win the last battle over Satan. Though psychology as a science is important, the Bible's primacy is undiminished.

PSYCHOLOGY AND THEOLOGY WORKING TOGETHER

Psychology (an evolving science based on observation of human behavior) and theology (the unchanging, God-revealed truths that inform faith and practice) can be complimentary. For example, the Bible is clear that God controls history. This is a vital truth found in the Bible, which the science of psychology is unable to detect through observation. I once worked with a very depressed woman whose main question had to do with who controlled the history of the world and her own history in particular. I was surprised by how many of her concerns were theological. We had many discussions about how her inaccurate theological beliefs were contributing to her depression.

MORE WAYS THEOLOGY AND PSYCHOLOGY CAN INTEGRATE

Sometimes the issues that get in the way of good theology are psychological (e.g., past abuse that makes a person unable to trust God). And sometimes what gets in the way of mental health is bad theology (e.g., not realizing how much God loves us). Helping hurting people sometimes requires us to draw on the truths of the Bible as well as psychology. The blue sky piece is that the cause of some mental health problems is spiritual. The green tree piece is that some illnesses, including mental health problems, are physically caused and cured. The puzzle fits together when we combine both possibilities. Some problems are both spiritual and physical, and treatment involves both spiritual and medical/psychological interventions.

HOW TO DO BOTH

In the thirty-ninth year of his reign, King Asa of Judah was afflicted with a disease in his feet. Though his disease was severe, he did not seek help from the LORD, only from physicians (2 Chronicles 16:12). The biblical record indicates that God was not concerned that he sought help from his doctors but that he did not seek help from the Lord. We need to do both.

SCIENCE IS IMPERFECT

Although it is possible for psychology and theology to be complimentary, sometimes they are not integrated. For example, some mental health professionals might support no-fault divorce, but God hates divorce (Malachi 2:16). Some mental health professionals might argue away guilt, but the Bible does not (Job 31:33). Some mental health professionals do not seek to integrate theology with science.

During my training I asked one of my supervisors why people should value themselves. He said that people should value themselves because they occupy space in the universe. His science was accurate: people do indeed occupy space. But he missed the theological truth found in the Psalms.

> You made [man] a little lower than the heavenly beings and crowned him with glory and honor. You made him ruler over the works of your hands; you put everything under his feet. (Psalm 8:5–6)

Some mental health professionals miss the ultimate truths. Psychology needs theology to be complete. In the same way, medicine needs theology to understand why abortion and euthanasia are wrong. Science is not the source of ultimate truths.

But just because psychology is incomplete does not mean it is a failure or useless. Psychology as a science describes what is seen, not what is unseen. To blame the science of psychology for not doing the work of theology is like disposing of a hammer because it can't bake bread.

Some Christians disregard psychology because Freud (1856–1939), the father of modern psychology, was anti-religion. But holding the entire science of psychology suspect because of Freud is like refusing to use medicine because Hippocrates, the Greek father of medicine, wasn't a Christian.

Psychology as a science has undergone significant change since its beginnings, and it continues to change based on research. Just as we continue going to the doctor even though medical knowledge is incomplete, we can enjoy the benefits of psychology even though it is an imperfect and growing science.

From the science of psychology, we learn that 90-95 percent of people who die by suicide have a diagnosable mental health problem. The science of psychology cannot predict who will die by suicide. But if I didn't know that a mental health problem was a risk factor for suicide, I would be less knowledgeable about how to prevent it.

PUZZLE: BOTH–AND

The blue sky piece—all mental health problems are spiritually caused and cured—and the green tree piece—health problems are physically caused and cured—can fit together. Mental health problems can have spiritual, physical, and psychological components. Both pieces can help to complete this puzzle. If you or someone you love is struggling with mental health issues, keep praying and consult a professional to determine if a physical or psychological component is part of the struggle.

FIND A GOOD PRACTITIONER WHO WILL RESPECT YOUR BELIEFS

We know from the science of psychology that people are more likely to get better if they have a good relationship with their practitioner. It's important to acknowledge that there are good and bad practitioners, including good non-

Christian practitioners and bad Christian practitioners. It's also important to note that we will get along better with some than with others.

Just as we shop for a good car mechanic or primary care doctor, so we need to shop for a good psychiatrist, psychologist, or counselor. Shopping can be a draining process. It can also be discouraging if we run into a bad practitioner. But one bad practitioner does not mean all are bad. Nor does one bad practitioner invalidate the whole field of psychology. One bad car mechanic doesn't mean that all car mechanics are bad, nor does it mean that the field of car mechanics is a bad profession.

Does the practitioner need to be a Christian? Just as a non-Christian doctor can be skilled and helpful, so a non-Christian psychologist can be helpful. It will be important, however, to be clear that you are a Christian. Be specific about your beliefs. Some Christians fear that a psychiatrist, psychologist, or counselor will manipulate a Christian's mind or impose incompatible values.

All professional ethical codes forbid manipulation or imposition of the practitioner's values onto the client. For example, Principle E of the American Psychological Association's Ethical Principles states:

> Psychologists are aware of and respect cultural, individual, and role differences, including those based on . . . religion . . . Psychologists try to eliminate the effect on their work of biases based on those factors, and they do not knowingly participate in

or condone activities of others based upon such prejudices.

If you are weighed down with depression or anxiety, pray and ask God for healing but also consider seeking help from a mental health professional who respects your Christian beliefs.

QUESTIONS FOR GROUP DISCUSSION OR PERSONAL REFLECTION

■ Give an example of how body, soul, and spirit are interrelated.

■ Do you agree or disagree that the Bible is all true but that not all truth is in the Bible? Why or why not?

■ How are theology and psychology interrelated?

■ If you sought counseling, would you seek a Christian practitioner? Why or why not?

My Hope

Rise to Power or Submit to the Powerful?

BLUE SKY

The LORD will make you the head, not the tail. If you pay attention to the commands of the LORD your God that I give you this day and carefully follow them, you will always be at the top, never at the bottom. (Deuteronomy 28:13)

GREEN TREE

A ruler who oppresses the poor is like a driving rain that leaves no crops.... When the righteous triumph, there is great elation; but when the wicked rise to power, men go into hiding.... Like a roaring lion or a charging bear is a wicked man ruling over a helpless people. (Proverbs 28:3, 12, 15)

COUNSELOR & CLIENT CONVERSATION

Me: We've been talking about depression being a sin. We've also talked about how you feel depressed when you're around your dad. Why is that?

CAROL: He criticizes me so much.

ME: And how does that turn into depression for you?

CAROL: His criticism creeps under my skin and I start to believe it. Maybe I really am worthless.

ME: How do you fight that creeping belief that maybe you really are worthless?

CAROL: One of the ways is that I keep telling him I'm a good person. I defend myself. But I'm not sure it's okay to do that if you're a Christian.

ME: So you wonder if it's okay to defend yourself and point out your good qualities?

CAROL: That's right.

ME: Why do you think it's wrong to defend yourself?

CAROL: Well, for one, you're supposed to just take it, turn the other cheek, but sometimes I criticize him back.

ME: So being criticized by your dad brings out the bully in you. And you're not sure if you want to be bullied or be the bully?

CAROL: Yes, I don't want to be either but I can't help being both!

WHEN I WAS GROWING UP IN FRANCE, ONE OF my neighbors, Thierry, bet me that French were better than Americans. Of course, I disagreed, so we set up an endurance race in the long parking lot of our apartment building to see who could complete one hundred laps. Back and forth I jogged until I was finally able to prove that Americans were just as good as the French. It was important to me to not be thought of as lesser than someone else. I've done many other things in my life to prove that I'm just as good as the next person.

Competitions are designed to show who is "the best." The results assign positions: top, middle, and bottom. Winning tells us "we're better." It sets up a natural pecking order. It's why hearing the U.S. national anthem at the Olympics brings tears of pride to our eyes.

No one, not even a very small dog, wants to be at the bottom. To find out where our three-pound Chihuahua, Choti, thought he fit in the family pecking order, my husband set up an experiment. He took away Choti's chew toy, and Choti just looked at the chew toy. Then I took it away. Again, he simply looked at the toy. Next, our oldest son took it away, and Choti still just looked at the toy. Finally, our youngest son (who weighed about forty times more than the dog) took away the chew toy. This time Choti growled and tried to get it back. Choti thought he was "one up" the pecking order from our youngest son.

The Israelites did not want to be the least of all their neighboring nations. God promised them that if they followed His commands, they would be at the top:

The LORD will make you the head, not the
tail. If you pay attention to the commands
of the LORD your God that I give you this
day and carefully follow them, you will
always be at the top, never at the bottom.
(Deuteronomy 28:13)

KICK OR BE KICKED

No one wants to be at the low end of the status ladder
because people who are there are subject to abuse. Abuse
trickles down toward the smaller and the more vulnerable.
The boss yells at you, you yell at your spouse, your spouse
yells at the kid, and the kid kicks the dog. The only person
immune from abuse is the person at the top.

Tales are full of unfair abuse and bullying. Cinderella's
stepmother and stepsisters forced Cinderella to sleep in the
cinders next to the fireplace and do drudgery work. Snow
White was banished to a forest cottage by her stepmother
who was jealous of her beauty. Oliver Twist was sold by the
workhouse caretakers.

Bullies also exist in real life. We encounter them in
the workplace, in families, in wars, in gangs. The movie
Sabrina is about a young girl working in Paris whose boss
kept asking her to do things she didn't understand or was
incapable of doing. She is given this advice: "I tortured your
boss and your boss is now torturing you. Do well, and then
you'll have someone of your own to torture." The rule of
abuse is that those at the top torture others. Those at the

bottom endure torture until they rise through the hierarchy so they can torture others.

King Solomon's son Rehoboam saw power as an opportunity to abuse others. His father had led Israel to a place of prominence and riches—but at a high price. He forced many Israelites into hard labor. When Rehoboam became king, the Israelites asked him to lighten their load. Instead, he said, "My little finger is thicker than my father's waist. My father laid on you a heavy yoke; I will make it even heavier. My father scourged you with whips; I will scourge you with scorpions" (1 Kings 12:11).

As a result, the people rebelled and Israel was split into the Northern Kingdom of Israel and the Southern Kingdom of Judah. This split occurred because of Rehoboam's promise to abuse power. The people of Israel wanted leadership, not abuse of power. Politicians are called "public servants" because their job is to serve their constituents' needs, not their own. And they are ultimately God's servants. Paul said, "For the authorities are God's *servants*, who give their full time to governing" (Romans 13:6). To Rehoboam, power was not an opportunity to serve his people but to serve his own desire (and that of his friends) for power. He saw power as either the blue sky piece of being at the top or the green tree piece of being at the bottom.

TURNING POWER UPSIDE DOWN

When Jesus entered time and space, He didn't talk about His right to power; He talked about being a servant. Jesus changed the prevailing "rules" of power when He said:

"You know that the rulers of the Gentiles lord it over them, and their high officials exercise authority over them. Not so with you. Instead, whoever wants to become great among you must be your servant, and whoever wants to be first must be your slave—just as the Son of Man did not come to be served, but to serve, and to give his life as a ransom for many." (Matthew 20:25-28)

Jesus modeled this teaching by demonstrating the proper use of power.

- He used powerful miracles to cement his claims to deity: "Even though you do not believe me, believe the miracles, that you may know and understand that the Father is in me, and I in the Father." (John 10:38)
- He used his power when he refused to be made a king prematurely: "Jesus, knowing that they intended to come and make him king by force, withdrew again to a mountain by himself." (John 6:15)
- He used his power to slip through hostile crowds. (Luke 4:30; John 8:59, John 10:39)
- He used his power as Lord of the universe to cast out demons. (Matthew 8:28–34)
- He used his power to give His life for ours.

Paul said that we're to use Jesus' model of power as our own:

> Your attitude should be the same as that of Christ Jesus: Who, being in very nature God, did not consider equality with God something to be grasped, but made himself nothing, taking the very nature of a servant, being made in human likeness. And being found in appearance as a man, he humbled himself and became obedient to death—even death on a cross! Therefore God exalted him to the highest place and gave him the name that is above every name, that at the name of Jesus every knee should bow, in heaven and on earth and under the earth, and every tongue confess that Jesus Christ is Lord, to the glory of God the Father. (Philippians 2:5–11)

Using power as Jesus did—to serve—prevents abuse.

The writer of Ecclesiastes recognized the corrosive potential of power:

> Again I looked and saw all the oppression that was taking place under the sun: I saw the tears of the oppressed—and they have no comforter; power was on the side of their oppressors—and they have no comforter. (4:1)

God pleaded with the powerful to not abuse their power:

This is what the Sovereign LORD says: "You
have gone far enough, O princes of Israel!
Give up your violence and oppression and
do what is just and right. Stop dispossessing
my people," declares the Sovereign LORD.
(Ezekiel 45:9)

The Israelites misused their power by taking advantage
of vulnerable people. God would not tolerate their
miscarriage of justice:

You who turn justice into bitterness and cast
righteousness to the ground . . . you hate
the one who reproves in court and despise
him who tells the truth. You trample on
the poor and force him to give you grain.
Therefore, though you have built stone
mansions, you will not live in them;
though you have planted lush vineyards,
you will not drink their wine. For I know
how many are your offenses and how great
your sins. You oppress the righteous and
take bribes and you deprive the poor of
justice in the courts. . . . But let justice roll
on like a river, righteousness like a never-
failing stream! (Amos 5:7, 10–12, 24)

The Bible addresses not only the plight of the abused
but also that of the abuser. God cares how people use
power, and sometimes He will remove it from those who

misuse it. The sons of Eli, Israel's priest, broke God's laws and threatened to take food by force if people didn't give it willingly (1 Samuel 2:16). They accepted bribes (1 Samuel 8:3). They slept with women other than their wives (1 Samuel 2:22). As a result, God took the priestly office away from Eli's family:

> Therefore the LORD, the God of Israel, declares: "I promised that your house and your father's house would minister before me forever." But now the LORD declares: "Far be it from me! Those who honor me I will honor, but those who despise me will be disdained. The time is coming when I will cut short your strength and the strength of your father's house, so that there will not be an old man in your family line." (1 Samuel 2:30–31)

"If a king judges the poor with fairness, his throne will always be secure" (Proverbs 29:14). The writer of this proverb understood that those who do not judge with fairness will lose their position of power. Sometimes God elevates the powerless to positions of power.

GOD EMPOWERS THE POWERLESS

The Bible gives many examples of God lifting the powerless to powerful positions.

Elkanah had two wives: Penninah and Hannah. Penninah

had children, and she made fun of Hannah who had none (1 Samuel 1:6). Penninah's meanness caused Hannah to cry and not eat (v. 7). The Bible describes her as being in "deep anguish," "weeping bitterly" (v. 10), and "pouring out her soul" to God (v. 15). Hannah wanted a child, and she wanted relief from Penninah. She cried out to God for help because she was powerless. God delivered her by giving her a son, Samuel, and then three more sons and two daughters (1 Samuel 2:21). God graciously gave this powerless woman a son who became one of Israel's most powerful figures.

Hannah's experience indicates that God decides who is powerful and who is not, that God notices the powerless and is gracious to them, that God respects the powerless, and that God can use the powerless as well as the powerful to accomplish His purposes. Hannah praises God for this:

> The LORD sends poverty and wealth; he humbles and he exalts. He raises the poor from the dust and lifts the needy from the dust; he seats them with princes and has them inherit a throne of honor . . . "It is not by strength that one prevails; those who oppose the LORD will be shattered."
> (1 Samuel 2:7–8, 9–10)

Mary the mother of Jesus was another woman who praised God for His regard for the powerless. He chose her, a lowly girl, to be the mother of the Messiah: "for he has been mindful of the humble state of his servant" (Luke 1:48).

HOW TO USE POWER WELL

I once received a promotion at work and became responsible for managing a large work group. My first impulse was to think what a great person I was! My second was to recognize that I could either use my power or abuse it.

British historian Lord Acton (1834–1902) said, "Power corrupts, and absolute power corrupts absolutely." Power is a seductive force that tempts us to use our position to abuse others. Morality sometimes decreases when power increases.

Jesus demonstrated the proper use of power. Even though Jesus knew that the Father had put "all things under his power," He performed the lowly task of washing His disciples' feet (John 13:3–5). A short time later, He submitted Himself to death on our behalf. Jesus taught us to do the same with our power: "Whoever wants to become great among you must be your servant" (Matthew 20:26).

Mother Teresa[31] followed Jesus' example. In 1950, she founded The Missionaries of Charity to love and care for the people others considered worthless. She loved the powerless, the disenfranchised, the poorest of the poor. Despite her own position of relative power as a Nobel Peace Prize winner, she cared for those who had no renown. She did this because Almighty God, the maker and ruler of the universe, set the example by caring for the most powerless.

POWER CAN BE GOOD

Used properly, power can change bad situations for the better. King Hezekiah's father was a morally corrupt king who shut down the temple and worshiped idols. But when Hezekiah became king at age twenty-five, he instituted reforms (2 Chronicles 29:1).

We don't have to be the leader of a nation to have power. Even "ordinary" people have the power to vote, to fight for justice, to support the oppressed and the disenfranchised. In whatever positions of power and influence we have, we can abuse our power or we can use it to serve those who have no power.

WHAT IS POWER?

One school of thinking[32] separates position power from personal power. Position power belongs to those who have a position of power (and responsibility) over others. Parents have position power over their children. Some parents shy away from taking hold of this power that is rightfully theirs. Parents don't have the right to abuse their children but they are entrusted with the power to take responsibility for them.

David recognized that God was the source of his position power.

> This is what the LORD Almighty says: "I took you from the pasture, and from following the flock to be ruler over my people Israel. I have been with you wherever you have gone, and I have cut off all your enemies from before you. Now I will make your name great, like the

names of the greatest men of the earth."
(2 Samuel 7:8–9)

Obadiah had position power as the person in charge of Ahab's palace. Ahab was one of Israel's most abusive kings. Obadiah used his position power to hide 100 prophets of the Lord from Ahab's wicked wife Jezebel, who was out to kill them. He used his power to do what was right.

Even those who have no position power have personal power. Personal power comes from the inside. Some people have personal power that comes from their ability to create a feeling of oneness in a group. Others have personal power stemming from special knowledge or an ability that others perceive as expertise. Others have personal power based on their ability to sell an idea or to convince others of its merits. Others have personal power that comes from their ability to motivate people.

The book of Ecclesiastes tells of a man with no position power who saved a city by using his personal power:

> I also saw under the sun this example of wisdom that greatly impressed me: There was once a small city with only a few people in it. And a powerful king came against it, surrounded it and built huge siegeworks against it. Now there lived in that city a man poor but wise, and he saved the city by his wisdom. (Ecclesiastes 9:13–15)

Even in positions of powerlessness, people have

personal power. Victor Frankl, incarcerated in a Nazi concentration camp in World War II, wrote these words about the power no one can take from us.

> We who lived in concentration camps can remember the men who walked through the huts comforting others, giving away their last piece of bread. They may have been few in number, but they offer sufficient proof that everything can be taken from a man but one thing: the last of human freedoms—to choose one's attitude in any given set of circumstances—to choose one's own way.[33]

While working in a situation where I felt powerless, I started a daily journal of God's goodness to me. Every night when I was brushing my teeth, I struggled to find something to thank God for in the midst of my bleak circumstances. Over time, I discovered that God's "compassions never fail" (Lamentations 3:22).

We all have the personal power to respond as God's servant to an abusive situation.

USING POWER TO SERVE OTHERS

In countless ways, we can use our power to serve others:

- We work hard to earn money to put our kids through school.

- We make nutritious meals to keep our family healthy.
- We listen to people when they are hurting.
- We take care of kids when parents need time off.
- We use our spiritual gifts and abilities to build up the church.
- We pray for those who need help from above.
- We speak the truth in love.
- We send a cheery card to those who need encouragement.
- We defend those who are being abused or bullied.
- We share our money with people who need it.
- We adopt an orphan.
- We join organizations that protect the vulnerable.
- We are just and righteous in all our dealings.
- We create a feeling of oneness in a group, share special knowledge or an ability, sell ideas or convince others of its merits, and use charisma to motivate others.
- Most of all, we make sure that the powerless are taken care of and that we never misuse power.

Nehemiah was governor over Jerusalem and was working to rebuild the city wall to keep the Israelites safe. He could have taken advantage of the Israelites in his position of power, but he chose not to because he wanted to do for others what he would have liked others to do for him.

Moreover, from the twentieth year of

King Artaxerxes, when I was appointed
to be their governor in the land of Judah,
until his thirty-second year—twelve
years—neither I nor my brothers ate the
food allotted to the governor. But the
earlier governors—those preceding me—
placed a heavy burden on the people and
took forty shekels of silver from them in
addition to food and wine. Their assistants
also lorded it over the people. But out of
reverence for God I did not act like that.
Instead, I devoted myself to the work on
this wall. All my men were assembled
there for the work; we did not acquire
any land. Furthermore, a hundred and
fifty Jews and officials ate at my table, as
well as those who came to us from the
surrounding nations. Each day one ox,
six choice sheep and some poultry were
prepared for me, and every ten days an
abundant supply of wine of all kinds. In
spite of all this, I never demanded the
food allotted to the governor, because
the demands were heavy on these people.
Remember me with favor, O my God,
for all I have done for these people.
(Nehemiah 5:14–19)

May we use our power well to take care of others in
need of our help.

ABUSE PREVENTION

My friend Monica was working for an administrator who was belittling her in meetings and sabotaging her work. Other teachers noticed and asked Monica if she was feeling beat up. She was! It took five years, but Monica finally mounted her courage and voiced her objections to the unfair and unjust treatment. She was too nervous to say it in person, so she wrote a letter. Monica cited examples of times in meetings when the administrator demeaned her. She described other occasions when the administrator had sabotaged her and her work. After giving the administrator the letter, she followed up with a conversation. And it worked! The administrator stopped her abusive behavior. Monica wishes she had been assertive long before!

If you've tried being assertive and have gotten nowhere (that happens!), or if you don't think you're ready to be assertive, or if you don't think you'll ever be ready to be assertive, find a way to manage the stress. When your sense of safety (physical or emotional) is threatened, stress hormones flood your body in preparation for assault. The positive side of these hormones is that they keep you alert and ready for action. The negative side is that you are chronically stressed. To avoid long-term effects, you need to take care of your body.[34] Drink a lot of water, eat nutritious foods, sleep eight hours every night (if your mind isn't going a thousand miles an hour!), and exercise. It's also important to manage all the emotions that are flooding your mind by talking to God, to a friend, and to a counselor.

If nothing improves (or if it gets worse), consider

leaving the situation. Consider all the possible ways to "leave," including setting boundaries or even separation. Stop calling the abusive family member, find a new job, or get a new friend.

HOW NOT TO PERPETUATE THE CYCLE OF ABUSE

One of the mysteries of life is why a person who has been abused becomes an abuser, but it sometimes happens. Such people seem to forget what being abused feels like. The writer of Proverbs tells us to tremble when a person who is "one down" becomes "one up."

> Under three things the earth trembles,
> under four it cannot bear up: a servant who
> becomes king, a fool who is full of food,
> an unloved woman who is married, and
> a maidservant who displaces her mistress.
> (Proverbs 30:21–23)

After being on the bottom for so long, some people are determined to rise to a position of power. One of the ways they enjoy their power is to abuse those under them.

If, despite being abused, you don't want to become an abuser, refuse to accept the view of power that says you're either the abuser or the abused. Instead, accept Jesus' perspective. Use power to serve others. As Jesus said, "So in everything, do to others what you would have them do to you, for this sums up the Law and the Prophets" (Matthew 7:12). Treat others the ways you wish you had been treated.

Doing good for someone who hurt you is a difficult task. You also need to work on forgiving the abuser. Forgiving "the bad guy" feels unfair. But forgiveness is essential.

Nelson Mandela said, "Resentment is like drinking poison and then hoping it will kill your enemies." A Chinese proverb says that the one who pursues revenge should dig two graves. In other words, revenge is bad for people on both ends of it. Modern science supports the truth of this ancient proverb. Research has found that holding onto resentment can result in high blood pressure, heart disease, cancer, headache, backache, ulcers, wrinkles, colds, flu, anxiety and depression.[35]

We can avoid the consequences of resentment by forgiving.

When my husband and I had been married almost a year, we helped with a beach camp in Karachi, Pakistan. A few weeks before the camp started, we were dropped off at a beautiful deserted beach (with no transportation back to civilization) to celebrate Christmas. I had some small gifts for my husband, but he hadn't yet thought about gifts. I was hurt because I thought love meant thinking ahead, and he was hurt because my resentment wrecked the Christmas spirit.

I conveniently forgot all the times that I had not planned ahead, and I took for granted the forgiveness I had received from God and others. I felt no obligation to pass along any of it to my husband.

The Bible tells us countless times to forgive others. "Bear with each other and forgive whatever grievances you may have against one another. Forgive as the Lord forgave you" (Colossians 3:13). In these commands to forgive, one of the most cited reasons is that *God has forgiven us.*

TAKING FORGIVENESS FOR GRANTED

When we travel overseas, I am reminded of how wonderful it is at home to enjoy clean, safe drinking water straight from the tap. I get used to having it; I even start to feel entitled to it! God's forgiveness is like water from the tap: we get so used to having it that we forget it's an ever-present gift that we should not take for granted. We need to constantly remind ourselves of how much God's forgiveness means to us so that we can forgive others.

The psalmist understood this and could hardly contain his praise for God because of his forgiven sin:

> Praise the LORD, O my soul;
>> all my inmost being, praise his holy name.
> Praise the LORD, O my soul,
>> and forget not all his benefits—
> who forgives all your sins
>> and heals all your diseases,
> who redeems your life from the pit
>> and crowns you with love and compassion,
> who satisfies your desires with good things
>> so that your youth is renewed like the eagle's.
> The LORD works righteousness
>> and justice for all the oppressed.
> He made known his ways to Moses,
>> his deeds to the people of Israel:

> The LORD is compassionate and gracious,
>   slow to anger, abounding in love.
> He will not always accuse,
>   nor will he harbor his anger forever;
> he does not treat us as our sins deserve
>   or repay us according to our iniquities.
> For as high as the heavens are above the earth,
>   so great is his love for those who fear him;
> as far as the east is from the west,
>   so far has he removed our transgressions
>   from us. (Psalm 103:1–12)

God not only removes our transgressions as far from us as the east is from the west, He also makes our scarlet sins as white as snow (Isaiah 1:18). He redeemed us through His blood (Ephesians 1:7), and purifies us from all unrighteousness (1 John 1:9). Recognizing God's forgiveness encourages us to forgive others.

Some people are weighed down and crushed under a burden of resentment and bitterness, but not Bishop Desmond Tutu. He worked with the Truth and Reconciliation Commission of South Africa to review the abuses of apartheid and to develop a reconciliation plan to bring together the whites who had abused power and the blacks who had suffered terrible atrocities. He wrote:

> Forgiving and being reconciled are not about pretending that things are other than they are. It is not patting one another on the back and turning a blind eye to the wrong.

True reconciliation exposes the awfulness, the abuse, the pain, the degradation, the truth. It could even sometimes make things worse. It is a risky undertaking but in the end it is worthwhile, because in the end dealing with the real situation helps to bring real healing. Spurious reconciliation can bring only spurious healing. . . . In forgiving, people are not being asked to forget. On the contrary, it is important to remember, so that we should not let such atrocities happen again. Forgiveness does not mean condoning what has been done. It means taking what happened seriously and not minimizing it; drawing out the sting in the memory that threatens to poison our entire existence. It involves trying to understand the perpetrators and so have empathy, to try to stand in their shoes and appreciate the sort of pressures and influences that might have conditioned them. . . . Forgiving means abandoning your right to pay back the perpetrator in his own coin, but it is a loss that liberates the victim. . . . True forgiveness deals with the past, all of the past, to make the future possible.[36]

Forgiveness is *not* condoning wrong behavior. Nor is it saying that what happened is okay. It is letting go of resentment and revenge.

Forgiving someone does not require that we allow their hurtful behavior to continue. In the parable of the unmerciful servant, where a king forgave the debts of a servant who then demanded that his fellow servant pay him back, the unmerciful servant's peers brought the unfairness to the attention of the king. The other servants "were greatly distressed and *went and told their master* everything that had happened" (Matthew 18:31, emphasis added). They made sure the unfairness did not continue.

ADMIT VALUE

When other people hurt us, we worry that we deserved to be treated badly; we wonder why we didn't see it coming; we feel inadequate for not being able to stop it from happening. But forgiving someone does not require that we admit having deserved abuse. No one deserves abuse. The road to forgiving begins with admitting our value.

God did not create infallible human beings. We have limitations that keep us from achieving perfection. Yet when God looked at us, His creation, He said, "It is very good" (Genesis 1:31).

In February 2005, Christie's of London sold a Henry Matisse painting of a piece of red seaweed on a blue background for over one million dollars.[37] Art is worth whatever someone is willing to pay for it.

Our worth is determined in the same way. If we think that our sin makes us any less loved and valued by God, think about the price He was willing to pay for us. We know what we are worth because of the exorbitant price

God paid for us: Jesus' death. God values us greatly; He has paid the ultimate price for us.

The severity of our sin does not lessen our value.

TRUST GOD

When our younger son was a child, he loved to be thrown up in the air and caught. As an adult, I don't have the trust to enjoy that kind of thing. Kids are good at trust. That's why Jesus used them as examples of trust (Matthew 18:1–3). Despite appearances to the contrary, God loves us. When we have no clue as to why He is doing certain things or allowing unpleasant things to happen, we have to trust Him as a child trusts a parent who is tossing him in the air.

Paul wrote: "Do not take revenge, my friends, but leave room for God's wrath, for it is written: 'It is mine to avenge; I will repay,' says the Lord" (Romans 12:19). God will avenge all the abuses we've suffered. The psalmist trusted God to avenge abuses against him:

> Before our eyes, make known among the nations
>> that you avenge the outpoured blood of your
>>> servants.
> May the groans of the prisoners come before you;
>> by the strength of your arm
>> preserve those condemned to die.
> Pay back into the laps of our neighbors seven
>> times
>> the reproach they have hurled at you, O LORD.
> Then we your people, the sheep of your pasture,

will praise you forever;
from generation to generation
we will recount your praise. (Psalm 79:10–13)

God promised vengeance on those who abuse power:

"So I will come near to you for judgment. I will be quick to testify against sorcerers, adulterers and perjurers, against those who defraud laborers of their wages, who oppress the widows and the fatherless, and deprive aliens of justice, but do not fear me," says the LORD Almighty. (Malachi 3:5)

Knowing that justice will be done can help us find the courage to forgive and to reconcile with others.

THE POWER PUZZLE

We started out looking for pieces of a puzzle that pictured only two options: be abused by those with power or use power to abuse others. But the picture Jesus is painting presents another option: use power to serve others. Even the weakest person has the power to do something good for someone else.

QUESTIONS FOR GROUP DISCUSSION OR PERSONAL REFLECTION

- What are some "one up" and "one down" relationships that you've been involved in?

- How do you stand up under someone who abuses their power?

- What can you do today to use your power to serve others?

- What is the hardest thing about forgiveness for you?

Putting the Pieces Together

LATE ONE RAINY, FOGGY NIGHT, MY HUSBAND AND I were driving over Red Mountain Pass between Ouray and Silverton, Colorado. Rocks were scattered all over the road, and there were no guardrails to keep us from falling hundreds of feet to the canyon floor below. Near the top of the pass, a mound of mud as high as our car slid down the mountain and across the road in front of us. We were stuck between the rocky road behind us and a mudslide in front of us. We didn't want to turn around, but we couldn't go forward.

Sometimes we get stuck in our Christian faith. We can get stuck when we can't figure out a puzzle. Some matters of Christian faith are easy to figure out, but others are not. When we come to a stuck place in our journey of faith, we first have to find out if we're dealing with a puzzle.

For example, the Bible is clear that Jesus was God's Son born of a young virgin woman (Luke 1:34–35), that He was fully divine (Luke 22:70), and that He died and was resurrected (Luke 24:5–8). The Bible presents no alternate way of looking at the historical Jesus. We either accept what it says or we don't.

But sometimes the Bible supports more than one side of an issue. For example, God created the world with cause and effect predictability, but He isn't limited by our expectations for predictability. According to the wisdom of Proverbs, "When a man's ways are pleasing to the LORD, he makes even his enemies live at peace with him" (16:7). This happened for Hezekiah, king of Judah (2 Kings 19:35), but not for Jesus. Jesus' enemies did not make peace with Him. In fact, they put Him to death. Does the example of Jesus nullify the principle in Proverbs? No. A principle can be generally true.

When we encounter seeming opposites that both have biblical support, we need to find the middle ground between them. We expect predictability, but we also expect God to interrupt our predictable lives. We also must make sure we have the right two opposites. For example, we think that we need to be perfect to merit God's love, but we get stuck in the reality of our imperfection. These pieces can create an unsolvable puzzle. We need new pieces. Once we have the right puzzle pieces we can solve the puzzle. We accept God's love for us as sinners (Ephesians 2:8–9), and we continue to work out our salvation (Philippians 2:12–13). Once we have the right pieces, we can fit the puzzles together.

THE PUZZLES

We put several puzzles together.
We discovered that we are to love others and ourselves.
We found that we are sinful yet wonderfully made.

We learned that God created the world with cause and effect predictably but He doesn't limit Himself to predictable behaviors. He is free to act however He wants.

We found that good and evil exist side by side.

We learned that we should seize some opportunities but let go at other times and let God move us forward according to His sovereign will.

We found that we have both strengths and weaknesses that can be used for God's glory.

We learned that we seek spiritual and physical solutions to our physical and mental health problems.

We also discovered that sometimes we are working with the wrong puzzle pieces. Instead of trying to make ourselves perfect to earn God's love, we learned that God loves us despite our imperfections on the basis of Christ's righteousness. In response to His love, we accept that we are sinful and imperfect, yet we work out our salvation by living holy lives to God. Although God loves us just as we are, we keep working to get better. And while we rest in God's love for us, we work out our salvation.

We found that when it comes to power structures, Jesus gives us new pieces. When we are powerful, we use our power to serve others. And when we are powerless, we serve others. The pieces fit together when we find ways to serve others from whatever position we are in.

BLUE, GREEN, AND IN BETWEEN

Opposites can fit together like the yolk and white of a sunny-side-up egg, or like heads and tails of a coin. We live in the tension between many opposing ideas, and we have to work to find middle ground. We need discernment to know when to claim our rights and when to give them up, when to seize an opportunity and when to wait for God's leading.

These questions require wisdom from God, which He has promised to give: "If any of you lacks wisdom, he should ask God, who gives generously to all without finding fault, and it will be given to him" (James 1:5).

This Puritan prayer captures the challenge of living in the tension between the paradoxical puzzle pieces of our faith:

> Lord, High and Holy, Meek and Lowly
> Thou hast brought me to the valley of
> vision, Where I live in the depths but
> see thee in the heights; Hemmed in by
> mountains of sin I behold thy glory. Let
> me learn by paradox
> > That the way down is the way up,
> > That to be low is to be high,
> > That the broken heart is the healed
> > > heart,
> > That the contrite spirit is the rejoicing
> > > spirit,
> > That the repenting soul is the
> > > victorious soul,
> > That to have nothing is to possess all,
> > That to bear the cross is to wear the
> > > crown,

> That to give is to receive,
> That the valley is the place of vision.
> Lord, in the daytime stars can be seen
> from the deepest wells, and
> The deeper the wells the brighter thy
> stars shine;
> Let me find thy light in my darkness,
> Thy life in my death,
> Thy joy in my sorrow,
> Thy grace in my sin,
> Thy riches in my poverty,
> Thy glory in my valley.[38]

As the Puritan prayed, ask God to give you the wisdom to learn how to live between these puzzling opposites. The writer of Ecclesiastes advises us to seek the middle ground:

> Do not be overrighteous, neither be overwise—why destroy yourself? Do not be overwicked, and do not be a fool—why die before your time? It is good to grasp the one and not let go of the other. The man who fears God will avoid all extremes. (Ecclesiastes 7:16–18)

TRUSTING GOD'S WISDOM

God has promised to provide wisdom, but the question

is, do we want the wisdom God gives? Do we trust Him? Once Jesus started making claims of divinity, many of His followers were offended and stopped following Him (John 6:66). After He claimed to have come from heaven, they no longer wanted to be associated with Him.

At times, we have similar feelings. When we hear His teaching on being a servant (Matthew 20:26), we might feel as if His teachings are too hard.

We might feel offended by what God does—or doesn't do. While traveling through New Dehli, India, I was overcome by the desperate poverty and couldn't help wondering why God didn't do something about it. When David saw wicked people hunting down the weak, he cried out, "Why, O LORD, do you stand far off? Why do you hide yourself in times of trouble?" (Psalm 10:1). In hard times, we question God. Some even turn away and don't want anything to do with Him.

Others respond like Peter, who said, "Lord, to whom shall we go? You have the words of eternal life. We believe and know that you are the Holy One of God" (John 6:68–69). We work out our puzzles with God because there's no other option. He is the only great God of the universe and He loves us. Where else can we go? Who else is as great? Who else loves us so much?

Job had differences with God. He wondered why God had inflicted him with so much pain. But God didn't love Job any less for his questions. In fact, God seems to have honored Job's efforts at deepening his relationship with God. God "made [Job] prosperous again and gave him twice as much as he had before" (Job 42:10).

We work to understand God just as two friends would work at understanding each other. After hearing God's response to Job's argument, Job said:

> "I know that you can do all things; no plan of yours can be thwarted. You asked, 'Who is this that obscures my counsel without knowledge?' Surely I spoke of things I did not understand, things too wonderful for me to know. (Job 42:2–3)

Like Job, may we make our home in God's just love and find rest for our souls. May we continue to deepen our understanding of the puzzles of our faith.

NOTES

1   The idea of syntheses, or looking at two opposites at the same time, has been around since the Greeks. Georg Hegel (1770–1831) popularized the idea of syntheses. He said there are many ideas that have opposites. Hegel called the first idea a Thesis and the opposite idea Antithesis. The Synthesis between the two opposites does justice to both. Another framework besides Hegel's puzzle is the concept of "apparent contradiction," which can be defined as a surface inconsistency or discrepancy or paradox.

2   Jean M. Twenge explores this subject in her book *Generation Me: Why Today's Young Americans Are More Confident, Assertive, Entitled—And More Miserable Than Ever Before* (New York: Free Press, 2006).

3   Edward F. Campbell, Jr., *Ruth: A New Translation with Introduction and Commentary* (Garden City, NY: Doubleday, 1975).

4   Desmond Tutu, *No Future without Forgiveness* (New York: Doubleday, 1999), 278–279.

5 Melody Beattie, *Codependent No More: How to Stop Controlling Others and Start Caring for Yourself* (San Francisco: Harper San Francisco, 1987).

6 Roger Fisher and William Ury, *Getting to Yes: Negotiating Agreement without Giving In* (Boston: Houghton Mifflin, 1981).

7 Cecil Adams, "The Straight Dope," http://www.straightdope.com/columns/040116.html.

8 Carl Bianco, "How Vision Works," http://science.howstuffworks.com/eye2.htm.

9 Douglas K. Detterman, "Intelligence and the Brain," P. A. Vernon, ed., *Handbook of the Neuropsychology of Individual Differences* (San Diego, CA: Academic Press, 1994) quoted in Jerome M. Sattler, *Assessment of Children Cognitive Applications*, 4th ed. (La Mesa, CA: Jerome M. Sattler Publisher, Inc., 2001) 161.

10 "How Do Artificial Flavors Work?" http://science.howstuffworks.com/question391.htm.

11 Quoted in Des McHale, Wisdom (London, 2002) http://www-gap.dcs.st-and.ac.uk/~history/Quotations/Newton.html.

12 Milton J. Erickson, *Christian Theology*, vol. 2 (Grand Rapids, Mich.: Baker Book House, 1984), 578.

13 See Mark R. McMin et al., "Professional Psychology and the Doctrines of Sin and Grace: Christian Leaders' Perspectives," *Professional Psychology: Research and Practice*, 37(3) (June 2006), 295–302.

14 Gracia Burnham, *In the Presence of My Enemies* (Wheaton, Ill., Tyndale, 2004) 228.

15 Dennis Linn, Sheila Fabricant Linn, & Matthew Linn, *Sleeping with Bread: Holding What Gives You Life* (Mahway, NY: Paulist Press, 1995).

16 Haddon W. Robinson, *Decision-Making by the Book* (Grand Rapids, Mich., Discovery House, 1998) 54–55.

17 Richard Nelson Bolles, *What Color Is Your Parachute?* (Berkeley, Calif.: Ten Speed Press, 1992) 395.

18 "The Twelve Steps of Alcoholics Anonymous," Step 3: "Made a decision to turn our will and our lives over to the care of God as we understood Him." http://www.alcoholics-anonymous.org.

19 Jean de la Fontaine, "Aide-toi, le ciel t'aidera." From "Le Chartier Embourbe" in *Les Fables* of Jean de la Fontaine.

20 St. Augustine, "Homily 7 on the First Epistle of John," http://www.newadvent.org/fathers/170207.htm.

21 "Shikarpur Diary: A Road Less Traveled," (Grand Rapids, Mich., *Day of Discovery*, RBC Ministries) http://www.rbc.org/radio_and_tv/day_of_discovery/32362.aspx.

22 S. G. Farnham, J. P. Gill, R. T. McLean, S. M. Ward, *Listening Hearts: Discerning Call in Community* (Morehouse Publishing, 1991).

23 "The Black Death Bubonic Plague during the Elizabethan Era," http://www.william-shakespeare.info/bubonic-black-plague-elizabethan-era.htm.

24 "The Black Death: Bubonic Plague," http://www.themiddleages.net/plague.html.

25 "The Black Death: The Flagellants," http://history.boisestate.edu/westciv/plague/13.shtml.

26 See P. D. Y. Trice and J. P. Bjorck, "Pentecostal Perspectives on Causes and Cures of Depression," *Professional Psychology: Research and Practice*, 37(3) (June 2006) 283–294.

27 U.S. Department of Health and Human Services. "Mental

Health: A Report of the Surgeon General" (1999), http://
mentalhealth.samhsa.gov/cmhs/surgeongeneral/larrysgr2.asp.

28 "Otto Loewi: The Nobel Prize in Physiology or Medicine
1936." From *Nobel Lectures, Physiology or Medicine 1922–1941*
(Amsterdam, Elsevier Publishing Company, 1965). http://
nobelprize.org/medicine/laureates/1936/loewi-bio.html

29 Stuart M. Butler et al., "Is Prayer Good for Your Health?
A Critique of the Scientific Research." The Heritage Foundation,
Heritage Lecture #816. http://www.heritage.org/Research/
Religion/HL816.cfm.

30 Arthur Holmes, *All Truth Is God's Truth* (Grand Rapids,
Mich., Eerdmans, 1977) 8.

31 "Mother Teresa: The Nobel Peace Prize 1979."
From Nobel Lectures, Peace 1971-1980, Editor-in-Charge
Tore Frängsmyr, Editor Irwin Abrams, World Scientific
Publishing Co., Singapore, 1997. http://nobelprize.org/peace/
laureates/1979/teresa-bio.html Retrieved April 27, 2006.

32 Developed by French and Raven. See B. H. Raven, "The
Bases of Power: Origins and Recent Developments," *Journal of
Social Issues* (1993) 49(4), 227–251. Later extended by G. Yukl
and C. M. Falbe, "Importance of Different Power Sources in
Downward and Lateral Relations" *Journal of Applied Psychology*,
76 (1991) 416–423.

33 Viktor E. Frankl, *Man's Search for Meaning* (New York:
Washington Square Press, Simon and Schuster, 1963) 104.

34 For more information go to the U.S. National Library of
Medicine and the National Institutes of Health, http://www.nlm.
nih.gov/medlineplus/stress.html.

35 Jordana Lewis and Jerry Adler, "Forgive and Let Live:
Revenge is sweet, but letting go of anger at those who wronged

you is a smart route to good health." *Newsweek*, September 27, 2006.

36 Tutu, *No Future without Forgiveness*, 270–271, 279.

37 Gallery of Highlights: Henry Matisse (1869–1954). http://www.christies.com/history/promo_gallery.asp?page=1.

38 Arthur G. Bennett, *The Valley of Vision: A Collection of Puritan Prayers and Devotions* (Carlisle, Penn.: Banner of Truth Trust, 1997).

NOTE TO THE READER

The publisher invites you to share your response to the message of this book by writing Discovery House Publishers, P.O. Box 3566, Grand Rapids, MI 49501, U.S.A. or by calling 1-800-653-8333. For information about other Discovery House publications, contact us at the same address and phone number.